Using Feedback
in Organizational
Consulting

Fundamentals of Consulting Psychology Book Series

Transcultural Competence: Navigating Cultural Differences in the Global Community
Jerry Glover and Harris L. Friedman

Using Feedback in Organizational Consulting
Jane Brodie Gregory and Paul E. Levy

APA FUNDAMENTALS OF CONSULTING PSYCHOLOGY

Using Feedback in Organizational Consulting

JANE BRODIE GREGORY AND PAUL E. LEVY

AMERICAN PSYCHOLOGICAL ASSOCIATION • *Washington, DC*

Published by
American Psychological Association
750 First Street, NE
Washington, DC 20002
www.apa.org

To order
APA Order Department
P.O. Box 92984
Washington, DC 20090-2984
Tel: (800) 374-2721; Direct: (202) 336-5510
Fax: (202) 336-5502; TDD/TTY: (202) 336-6123
Online: www.apa.org/pubs/books
E-mail: order@apa.org

In the U.K., Europe, Africa, and the Middle East, copies may be ordered from
American Psychological Association
3 Henrietta Street
Covent Garden, London
WC2E 8LU England

Typeset in Minion by Circle Graphics, Inc., Columbia, MD

Printer: Maple Press, York, PA
Cover Designer: Naylor Design, Washington, DC

The opinions and statements published are the responsibility of the authors, and such opinions and statements do not necessarily represent the policies of the American Psychological Association.

Library of Congress Cataloging-in-Publication Data

Gregory, Jane Brodie.
 Using feedback in organizational consulting / Jane Brodie Gregory and Paul E. Levy.
  pages cm. — (Fundamentals of consulting psychology book series)
 Includes bibliographical references and index.
 ISBN 978-1-4338-1951-3 — ISBN 1-4338-1951-1 1. Feedback (Psychology)
2. Communication in organizations. 3. Organizational effectiveness. 4. Organizational behavior. 5. Psychology, Industrial. I. Levy, Paul E. (Paul Edgar), 1962- II. Title.
 BF319.5.F4G74 2015
 001—dc23
                                    2014043623

British Library Cataloguing-in-Publication Data
A CIP record is available from the British Library.

Printed in the United States of America
First Edition

http://dx.doi.org/10.1037/14619-000

Contents

CONTENTS

Series Editor's Foreword

Rodney L. Lowman

The field of consulting psychology has blossomed in recent years. It covers the applications of psychology in consultation to organizations and systems but also at the individual and team levels. Unfortunately, there are very few graduate training programs in this field of specialization, so consulting psychology roles are mostly populated by those who came to the field after having trained in other areas of psychology—including industrial–organizational (I-O), clinical/counseling, and school psychology, among others. Yet such training is rarely focused on consulting psychology and psychologists, and graduate students have to learn through on-the-job training and by reading books and articles, attending conferences and workshops, and being mentored in the foundational competencies of the field as they seek to transition into it.

After a number of years of editing *Consulting Psychology Journal: Practice and Research*, the field's flagship journal, I felt that an additional type of educational product was needed to help those transitioning into consulting psychology. The Society of Consulting Psychology therefore partnered with the American Psychological Association and worked with an advisory board (initially consisting of Drs. Judith Blanton, Dale Fuqua, Skipton Leonard, Edward Pavur, Jr., and myself) to create a new book series describing the specific, fundamental skill sets needed to practice in this area of specialization. Our goal in this book series has been to identify the major competencies needed by consulting psychologists and then to work with qualified authors to create short, accessible but evidence-based texts that would be useful both as stand-alone volumes and in combination with one another. The readers would be graduate students in relevant training programs, psychologists planning a transition into consulting psychology, and practicing professionals who want to add to their areas of expertise.

What constitutes fundamental skills in consulting psychology? The educational guidelines created by the Society of Consulting Psychology and approved by the American Psychological Association (2007) and the *Handbook of Organizational Consulting Psychology* (Lowman, 2002) provide useful starting points. Both of these contributions were organized around the concept of levels (individual, group, and organizational) as a taxonomy for identifying fundamental skills. Within those categories, two broad skill sets are needed: assessment and intervention.

As with many areas of psychological practice, the foundational skills that apply in one area may overlap into others in the taxonomy. Interventions with individuals, as in executive coaching, for instance, usually take place in the context of the focal client's work with a specific team and within a specific organization, which itself may also constitute a client. Understanding the system-wide issues and dynamics at the organizational level usually also involves work with specific executives and teams. And multicultural/international issues suffuse all of our roles. The APA Guidelines and the *Handbook* concluded, properly, that consulting psychologists need to be trained in and have at least foundational skills and experience at the individual, group, and organizational levels, even if they primarily specialize in one of these areas.

In inviting you to learn more about consulting psychology through this book series, I hope you will come to agree that there is no more exciting or inherently interesting area of study today than consulting psychology. The series aims not only to cover relevant literature on timeless topics in consulting psychology but also to capture the richness of this work by including case material that illustrates its applications. Readers will soon understand that consulting psychologists are real-world activists, unafraid to work in real-world environments.

Finally, as one who trained in both I-O and clinical psychology, I should note that consulting psychology has been the one area in which I felt that all of my training and skill sets were both welcome and needed.

And in a world where organizations and the individuals and teams within them greatly need help in functioning effectively; in bridging individual, group, and organization-level needs and constituencies; and in coping with the rapid expansion of knowledge and escalating competition and internationalization, this book series aims to make a difference by helping more psychologists join the ranks of qualified consulting psychologists. Collectively, we can influence not only an area of specialization in psychology, but also the world.

ABOUT THIS BOOK

If you are an organizational consultant, chances are high that you will be spending a good part of your career providing and receiving feedback. And if you are a consulting psychologist—or learning to become one—you will want to know what the research literature has to say about what works best and why and what needs to be avoided.

Gregory and Levy's *Using Feedback in Organizational Consulting* is not a simple "how to" book—though it includes plenty of practical suggestions. Rather, it is a synthesis of what the applied process of giving feedback looks like when integrated with the research literature. It is, therefore, a great guide for evidence-based practice and as such a perfect volume for the Fundamentals of Consulting Psychology series.

How difficult can it be, a novice might understandably wonder, to provide effective feedback? Gregory and Levy make clear that there are many moving parts to providing effective feedback, including the nature and valence of the message, the feedback recipient, and the feedback giver. It is not all that easy to provide effective feedback, particularly when balancing all the elements of feedback while also addressing difficult problems in performance, interpersonal behavior, or character. Not too many consultants—much less supervisors—particularly relish the task of providing feedback. It can be emotionally demanding, and the outcomes are not always predictable. Even positive feedback is not always easy to provide well, because it may also need to include areas requiring attention. Too often the feedback provided is at too intense a level, with little sensitivity to the devastating effects it may be having on the recipient, or, conversely, at too superficial a level, such that the recipient goes away thinking everything is proceeding smoothly when in fact there are problems. Staying on message while also being sensitive to the emotional well-being of the person receiving the feedback, yet not pretending issues are not serious or do not need the person's attention, is, like much of the consulting craft, an art that is learned over time. The psychological casualties of providing feedback badly (e.g., too much negative feedback) may have the paradoxical effect of causing problematic behavior to worsen (see, e.g., Nowack & Mashihi, 2012).

These are just some of the reasons why consulting psychologists can be well suited to this competency and why this book is so valuable, important, and timely. Yet this book will be useful for others, as well. Providing effective feedback is an important managerial competency and, increasingly, psychologists are assuming managerial roles. For all of those who are called on to provide work-related feedback to others, Gregory and Levy's book will be a valuable, practical resource for years to come.

REFERENCES

American Psychological Association. (2007). Guidelines for education and training at the doctoral and postdoctoral levels in consulting psychology/organizational consulting psychology. *American Psychologist, 62*, 980–992. http://dx.doi.org/10.1037/0003-066X.62.9.980

Lowman, R. L. (Ed.). (2002). *The California School of Organizational Studies handbook of organizational consulting psychology: A comprehensive guide to theory, skills, and techniques.* San Francisco, CA: Jossey-Bass.

Nowack, K. M., & Mashihi, S. (2012). Evidence-based answers to 15 questions about leveraging 360-degree feedback. *Consulting Psychology Journal: Practice and Research, 64*, 157–182. http://dx.doi.org/10.1037/a0030011

Acknowledgments

It takes a village to raise a child, but you may not realize that it also takes a village to write a book. We are grateful to a number of friends and colleagues for their input and assistance with the development of this project. James Beck, Lauren Borden, Alison Gabriel, Katie Lotterman, Yoshi Nakai, Alison O'Malley, Elizabeth Pears, and Chris Rosen each provided valuable inputs and perspectives on portions of the book. We are grateful to our editor, Rodney Lowman, for the opportunity, his detailed and valuable feedback, and his direction along the way. We are also indebted to the American Psychological Association editorial team that helped us develop and improve our initial manuscript. Our unique figures represent the great work of *The Girl Tyler* (http://www.thegirltyler.com/), a talented graphic artist. Finally, we have both been supported by wonderful families throughout our personal and professional lives, and we thank them specifically for their support on this project. We owe them a great deal of gratitude for their continuing patience and support.

Using Feedback
in Organizational
Consulting

Introduction

Feedback is everywhere. Each of us gets it from our colleagues, friends, family members, and sometimes from random people on the street. We get it from tasks, machines, and the world around us. Most feedback is self-generated and appears consistently in our inner monologue as we assess and regulate our behavior throughout the day. It reflects reactions to and outcomes of our actions and behaviors, and it can come in verbal and written forms—and even in our observations of others' behaviors and expressions, which convey their reactions.

This book provides evidence-based best practices on how to give, receive, and help others deliver feedback in the most effective way possible. We present a straightforward model of the feedback process that is easily applied to practice and draws from decades of consistent findings in the feedback research. This model includes four critical elements of

http://dx.doi.org/10.1037/14619-001
Using Feedback in Organizational Consulting, by J. B. Gregory and P. E. Levy

any feedback exchange: (1) the feedback provider's actions and behaviors, (2) the content of the message, (3) the feedback recipient's beliefs and perceptions, and (4) the context in which feedback is provided. Although consulting psychologists are the intended audience for this book, the concepts presented are also useful to organizational consultants, managers, human resources (HR) professionals, and consultants with nonpsychology backgrounds.

Feedback plays a particularly important role in the work of consulting psychologists. According to the Society of Consulting Psychology (Division 13 of the American Psychological Association; http://www.apadivisions.org/division-13/index.aspx), consulting psychologists may work with individuals, groups, and organizational units, depending on the need and scope of the work. The goal of consulting psychology is to help individuals and organizations "become more efficient and effective" (Kurpius, 1978, p. 335). The work of consulting psychologists can take a variety of forms, and individuals who identify as consulting psychologists occupy a number of different roles.

Meet four consultants who appear throughout the following chapters:

- Lane is an internal consultant for a Fortune 100 organization and has a doctorate in industrial–organizational psychology. She designs systems and processes, and provides best practice guidance to HR professionals throughout this global organization. As part of the HR function, she consults widely with HR managers across business units and functions. The focus of her work varies based on business needs and priorities, but she has worked on the organization's annual employee engagement survey, talent management and performance management processes, and learning and development programs.
- Ted works for a large global consulting firm and is considered an expert on organization design, change, transformation, and effectiveness. He is often pulled into projects that focus on less macro topics; however, organizational design, change, and transformation are his areas of passion and expertise. Ted first completed a master's degree in counseling psychology and, later, when he realized how much he enjoyed working in the business world, pursued a master of business administration, with a focus on organizational behavior.

- Helen and Sylvia often collaborate on projects, although Helen is an independent executive coach and Sylvia works for a small firm that specializes in individual assessment. They met in graduate school, where Helen pursued a doctor of psychology in clinical psychology and Sylvia, a doctorate in consulting psychology.

Although the nature of their work varies slightly, these four consulting psychologists find that feedback is an essential part of their day-to-day business. The focus of that feedback, goal of delivering the feedback, type and frequency of the feedback, and feedback recipients vary from situation to situation; regardless of the context, though, feedback is a critical source of information.

Throughout the following eight chapters, we look closely at the essential role that feedback plays in helping organizations and the individuals within those organizations perform more effectively and efficiently. Chapter 1 provides a quick overview of what we consider to be classic models of feedback in organizations; those models have been most influential in the research and practice of feedback over the past several decades. They introduce critical concepts, such as the important role of individual differences and context in the feedback process, which are discussed in more detail later in the book. In Chapter 2, we explore a foundational theory about feedback processes in goal striving and behavior change: *control theory*, which suggests that feedback is the only way to gauge the gap or distance between our current state and goal state—where we are versus where we want to be. Chapters 3 and 4 get into the specifics of the feedback message itself and how it is delivered. For instance, not only does *what* we say matter, so does *how* we say it. Chapters 5 and 6 provide an overview of the role of individual differences and context in the feedback process. By *individual differences*, we mean unique characteristics that make us who we are, such as personality, motivation, and preferences. *Context* refers to aspects of the organizational environment that impact the feedback process. Chapter 7 focuses on the role of feedback in broader talent management processes, such as performance management, assessment, and coaching. Chapter 8 provides specific recommendations for using feedback in practice and research, and concluding thoughts.

We have structured each chapter to provide an overview of the most essential research and theory on the focal topic, but we also have made a point to discuss this research and theory in terms that are accessible and engaging to our readers. We then focus on the relevance and implications of that research to the workplace by presenting a case study[1] featuring one or more of the four consultants—Lane, Ted, Helen, and Sylvia. Our goal is to not only provide you with a foundation in the most essential feedback research and theory but to arm you with actionable and useful ideas for improving the way you approach feedback in your daily work as a consultant.

---

[1]Although our case studies are based on real-life events, the names of the consultants and some case details have been altered to respect confidence and privacy.

1

Laying the Foundation: Classic Models of Feedback in Organizations

Before introducing our new model or making recommendations for practice, it is important to review influential models of the feedback process that laid the foundation for the past several decades of feedback research. We begin with Ilgen, Fisher, and Taylor's (1979) model of individual feedback behavior in organizations, which later evolved into another model of individual reactions to feedback by the same authors (Taylor, Fisher, & Ilgen, 1984). Next, we discuss Kluger and DeNisi's (1996) feedback intervention theory (FIT), followed by London and Smither's (2002) model of the feedback process, which emphasizes the importance of context and individual differences. These models build on one another and inspired our simplified model of the feedback process, which is presented at the end of the chapter.

http://dx.doi.org/10.1037/14619-002
Using Feedback in Organizational Consulting, by J. B. Gregory and P. E. Levy
Copyright © 2015 by the American Psychological Association. All rights reserved.

ILGEN ET AL. (1979): INDIVIDUAL FEEDBACK BEHAVIOR IN ORGANIZATIONS

When they presented their model of the feedback process for individuals in organizations (see Figure 1.1) in their 1979 paper, Daniel Ilgen, F1 Cynthia Fisher, and Susan Taylor set the course for decades of feedback research that would follow. That model was the first of its kind: Although earlier research had examined feedback, no model had yet strung together the key influences that shape the feedback process. Ilgen et al. broke the feedback process into three component parts: (1) the source of the feedback, (2) actual feedback message, and (3) feedback recipient. They also explored important moderators that impact the feedback process and discussed outcomes that, based on the unique elements of a given feedback event, could result.

Beginning on the far left of the model, Ilgen et al. (1979) were quick to point out that all feedback comes from some source. Most often, we think about other people as the feedback source, but a feedback source can include oneself, the environment, or a task. For the purposes of this book, we have focused on feedback coming from other individuals. Consultants themselves could be a feedback source; when working with a client,

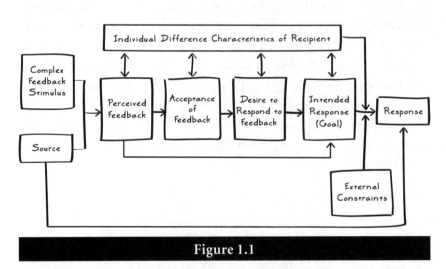

Figure 1.1

Ilgen et al.'s (1979) model of the effects of feedback on the recipient.

other feedback sources might include managers, business partners, direct reports, clients, customers, and others. It is important, though, to be aware that individuals also frequently self-generate feedback. For example, when an author reads a report and realizes that revisions are necessary, that realization is a form of self-generated feedback. Keep in mind that the environment is a rich source of feedback. When looking at a clock, for instance, and realizing that one is behind schedule and needs to speed up a work project, that clock is a critical source of feedback. When a client reviews annual goals and finds that progress toward the goals is less than desired, the client is generating feedback for himself or herself. As a consultant, it is important to recognize that clients are likely dealing with formal feedback received from others and self-generated feedback.

Certain characteristics of the feedback source affect how the recipient processes and interprets feedback. The credibility of the source has a substantial effect on how feedback is interpreted. Ilgen et al. (1979) identified two components of source credibility: expertise and trustworthiness. To be perceived as credible, a source must possess relevant expertise in the topic area of the feedback and must be deemed trustworthy by the recipient. Attributes of the feedback source—such as credibility—are discussed in greater detail in Chapter 4.

According to this model, feedback is generally either *directional*, that is, it provides clear direction on behaviors that the recipient should perform, or it is *motivational*, that is, it provides information about rewards associated with particular behaviors or outcomes (Ilgen et al., 1979). Ilgen and colleagues suggested that feedback needs to be conveyed to recipients in a way they can understand—in familiar terms that have clear informational value.

Referring to Figure 1.1, four steps play a role in how the recipient chooses to respond to the feedback. The first is how the recipient perceives or interprets the feedback and is reminiscent of the adage "perception is reality." That is, the feedback source may attempt to communicate one thing, but the subjective interpretation of that message is what is really "heard" by the recipient. The source's credibility influences how accurate the recipient believes the feedback to be. In addition, elements of the message impact how the recipient perceives it. Ultimately, the recipient's perception of the feedback determines whether he or she accepts the feedback. Feedback recipients' personal characteristics or individual differences influence every step of the model, including whether they are likely to accept the feedback. Such relevant individual differences are explored in greater detail in Chapter 5. If the recipient rejects the feedback, he or she may feel no impetus to respond or take action. However, once accepting the feedback, the recipient will likely respond to it in some way. How people respond to feedback varies based, in part, on their personality and individual tendencies.

Furthermore, the desire to respond to feedback depends on the same critical elements of the feedback process: the source, the message itself, and individual differences of the recipient. Whereas source credibility is vital to the recipient's perception of the feedback, the source's power comes into play regarding the recipient's desire to respond to feedback (Ilgen et al., 1979). The more power and influence the source has over rewards and outcomes, the more inclined the recipient should be to respond to or use the feedback.

Ilgen et al. (1979) suggested that three elements of the feedback message influence the recipient's desire to respond: (1) the timing of the feedback, (2) frequency with which feedback is given, and (3) the sign (positive or negative valence) of the feedback. These elements are discussed in greater detail in Chapter 3, but, in brief, Ilgen and colleagues noted that "reinforcing" feedback (e.g., positive) contributes to a desire to respond, as does feedback with strong informational value (e.g., tells the recipient that goals have been achieved or that changes in performance are needed). The authors touched on the role of frequency of feedback (e.g., the more often feedback is given, the more likely recipients will respond), which is a fundamental part of our discussion of the feedback environment (see Chapter 6). The nuances of the feedback message—such as how the message is perceived and whether the recipient will respond—that were discussed in Ilgen et al.'s work laid a foundation for several decades of important follow-up research as subsequent authors attempted to pinpoint the specific conditions under which feedback does or does not drive behavior change.

Individual differences play an important role in whether a recipient will respond to feedback. Ilgen et al. (1979) highlighted the importance of intrinsic motivation; self-efficacy, which they describe as an individual's beliefs about his or her response capability; and locus of control. Drawing on expectancy theory (Campbell & Pritchard, 1976; Vroom, 1964), the authors suggested that one important prerequisite to responding was whether recipients believed themselves capable of adequately responding to the feedback. Similarly, recipients must feel some degree of motivation to actually respond to the feedback. Two important ingredients of motivation to respond include a sense of competence (e.g., belief that the recipient possesses the necessary skills and capability to take action) and a sense of personal control over the situation (Deci, 1975). Similarly, the recipient's locus of control (internal vs. external) has important implications for whether he or she will respond to feedback. Ilgen et al. drew on a body of work from R. M. Baron (R. M. Baron, Cowan, & Ganz, 1974; R. M. Baron & Ganz, 1972), which demonstrated that individuals with an internal locus of control are more likely to respond to feedback, because taking action feeds their desire for learning and need for achievement. Individuals with an internal locus of control are more inclined to feel as if they have control over the situation and, therefore, their attempt at taking action will yield desirable results. Those findings led to a stream of research that focused on the importance of individual differences—such as implicit person theory and feedback orientation—which are the focus of Chapter 5.

Next, we consider more of Ilgen, Taylor, and Fisher's work as one of our foundational models of the feedback process. A few years later, these three authors followed up their original model with new theories that focused heavily on recipient reactions to feedback (Taylor et al., 1984). That model adopted a control theory perspective, which is discussed in greater detail in Chapter 2.

TAYLOR ET AL. (1984): INDIVIDUAL REACTIONS TO FEEDBACK

Taylor et al. (1984) drew on their earlier model as a foundation but focused on additional contingencies that impact how likely feedback recipients are to accept feedback. One significant contribution of this model was the authors' reliance on control theory as a framework for understanding the feedback process. Control theory suggests that we have some goal, standard, or desired state for our behavior—something we are working toward. Feedback allows us to gauge the distance between that standard and our current behavior (Carver & Scheier, 1998; Gregory, Beck, & Carr, 2011; Taylor et al., 1984). A model of control theory is featured in Figure 1.2. Control theory provides a simple and relevant framework for thinking about feedback and the important informational role it plays in the process of goal-striving and performance, a topic that is explored throughout this book.

According to Taylor et al. (1984), when feedback indicates a discrepancy between the standard and current performance, several reactions may follow. The feedback recipient could simply ignore the feedback or discrepancy and carry on as usual. The recipient could accept the feedback just enough to assess the accuracy of the discrepancy—in a sense, calibrating his or her perspective with that of the feedback source, which, in turn, could lead to a change in behavior, thereby reducing the discrepancy. The feedback recipient could discount the source's perspective, perhaps citing that he or she disagrees either with the standard or the current level of performance. The recipient could change or abandon the standard

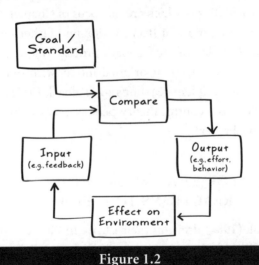

Figure 1.2

A simple control loop.

altogether (e.g., if not invested in the standard or goal, if the recipient does not believe the standard or goal is attainable or worth pursuing). One challenge often encountered in the workplace is that the feedback recipient does not always set the standard or goal, which, at times, can lead to conflict or disagreement about the standard, priorities, or expectations (Taylor et al., 1984). Taylor et al. suggested that individuals are most inclined to make comparisons between their own behavior and the standard when that standard is personally important or valuable. Thus, when someone else sets the standard, an individual's level of buy-in or commitment to that standard may not be as strong as it would if he or she had set the standard.

Taylor et al. (1984) outlined important moderators that affect how feedback recipients will respond to and subsequently take action on feedback based on this control theory perspective. One such moderator is the perceived accuracy of feedback. Feedback recipients are much more likely to accept and take action on feedback (e.g., comparing their current performance with the standard) when they perceive it to be an accurate assessment of their performance. Agreement on what the standard or goal is (i.e., a match in expectations) between the feedback source and the recipient increases the likelihood that a recipient will accept and act on the feedback. In addition, the recipient's attributions for the discrepancy play an important role in the person's reactions to and acceptance of feedback. For example, if negative feedback indicates that progress toward the standard or goal is happening too slowly, recipients may be able to attribute that slow pace to their own actions or perhaps to circumstances beyond their control—such as delays in getting important work or input from other stakeholders, adoption of new technology that has delayed work, or a massive snowstorm. Another important moderator draws on Ilgen et al.'s (1979) work, which highlighted the importance of the feedback source. Taylor et al. again emphasized the critical role of the source's trustworthiness and credibility in participant reactions to and acceptance of feedback. The last two moderators also drew on the Ilgen et al. model: feedback sign (positive or negative) and individual differences of the recipient; both moderators are discussed extensively in Chapters 3 and 5, respectively.

Like Ilgen et al. (1979), the Taylor et al. (1984) model provided a fundamental foundation for much of the feedback research that followed in the past several decades. The Taylor et al. model built seamlessly off the Ilgen et al. model, and both models have contributed to the backbone of theory for this book. Two additional models of feedback that have drawn on the work of these three authors are also important: Kluger and DeNisi (1996) introduced FIT, which helped to further clarify some of the idiosyncratic findings of Taylor et al.'s work. London and Smither's (2002) model blazed new territory for the role of feedback in the broader performance management process and also was the catalyst for subsequent research on the role of context (i.e., feedback culture or environment) and one specific individual difference: feedback orientation (Linderbaum & Levy, 2010).

KLUGER AND DENISI (1996): FIT

FIT was motivated, in part, by the inconsistent findings regarding the effectiveness of feedback—particularly negative feedback. Kluger and DeNisi (1996) suggested that the impact of feedback on behavior change is variable and often has little to no effect on subsequent behavior. As much as 38% of the time, feedback interventions even have an adverse effect on behavior and result in worse performance. In introducing FIT (see Figure 1.3), Kluger and DeNisi also drew heavily on control theory and set out to tease apart the unique elements of feedback that would make it more or less likely to have a positive effect on behavior.

FIT makes five basic arguments. The first draws heavily on control theory and states that behavior is regulated by the comparison of feedback to standards or goals. Second, goals are organized hierarchically (also a tenet of control theory; see Lord & Levy, 1994), meaning that goals range from being self-focused and abstract (higher order) to very basic tasks. Third, FIT posits that only the feedback/standard discrepancies that the individual pays attention to will result in behavior change. Fourth, attention is most often directed at goals at the moderate level of the goal hierarchy (not too high level or too specific). Fifth, feedback interventions can quickly and dramatically change the focus of attention and, therefore, behavior.

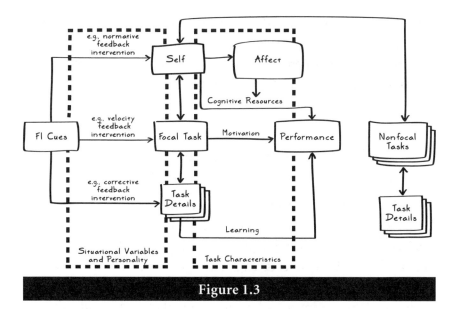

Figure 1.3

An overview of Kluger and DeNisi's (1996) FIT.

Attention to the self, as opposed to the task, tends to be more powerful. If an individual is focused on a task, but feedback diverts the person's attention to the self, the individual's attention will immediately shift to the self, thereby activating a sense of self-consciousness and distracting the individual from the task at hand.

Kluger and DeNisi's (1996) FIT is another seminal model of the feedback process in organizations, including the impact of the feedback source, message, and recipient on the effectiveness of the feedback process. The chapters that follow revisit the elements of FIT. All three of these key contributions to the literature (Ilgen et al., 1979; Kluger & DeNisi, 1996; Taylor et al., 1984) built on each other and influenced London and Smither's (2002) seminal work on modeling the feedback process in performance management. Although London and Smither drew on the work of these authors, they also highlighted an important gap in the literature: the failure to examine feedback in the broader context of work. Although the earlier models shaped our current understanding of the critical "ingredients" of feedback, they tended to examine feedback in a vacuum—as a stand-alone event. In reality, the feedback process occurs in the ongoing context of individual experiences, relationships, and work expectations. Thus, the fourth model presented as the "foundation" for our approach to feedback is London and Smither's (2002) model of feedback in the performance management process (see Figure 1.4).

LONDON AND SMITHER (2002): FEEDBACK IN THE PERFORMANCE MANAGEMENT PROCESS

In London and Smither's (2002) model, the individual first receives feedback from a source. Three stages follow: (1) receiving the feedback and having initial emotional reactions to it; (2) mindfully processing the feedback, which includes choosing to accept or reject the feedback; and (3) taking action on the feedback, for example, by setting goals for behavior change. If the recipient accepts the feedback, this three-step process can result in behavior change, such as enhanced performance or increased self-awareness. However, the process is subject to individual differences and contextual influences. An important contribution of London and Smither's (2002) model was their discussion of the impact of context on the feedback process. They introduced the concept of a feedback environment or culture that can influence every stage of the feedback process. Feedback environment can be conceptualized as the norms within an organization (or smaller unit, e.g., a department or team) for seeking feedback, providing feedback to others, encouraging others to seek and act on feedback, and holding employees accountable for acting on feedback that they receive (London & Smither, 2002; see also Steelman, Levy, & Snell, 2004). An organization's feedback environment is shaped largely by leaders within the organization who set the tone for how employees are expected to act when it comes to giving, receiving, and using feedback. Thus, the feedback environment within a given organization can have significant bearing on all three of London and Smither's (2002) stages of the feedback process: how individuals initially react to and receive feedback, how they interpret feedback when given time to mindfully process it, and whether they act on the feedback—and in what way.

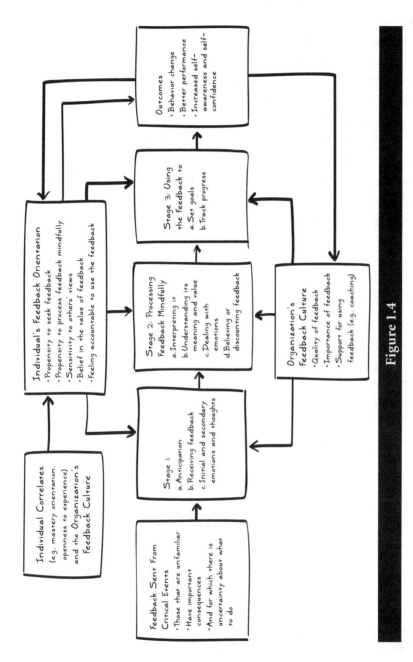

Figure 1.4

London and Smither's (2002) model of feedback in the performance management process.

Another significant contribution from London and Smither's model was the introduction of individual feedback orientation. Feedback orientation is an individual difference variable that impacts how individuals feel about the feedback (London & Smither, 2002; see also Linderbaum & Levy, 2010). Individuals with a favorable feedback orientation tend to be more open and receptive to feedback. They are more likely to welcome feedback, to proactively seek it out, and to value and act on the feedback they receive. Feedback orientation can be shaped or influenced by the feedback environment and other events and experiences. In addition, individuals' feedback orientations can influence the feedback environment with time; the relationship between these two constructs is reciprocal. Chapter 5 focuses heavily on feedback orientation.

CONCLUSION

These four models (Ilgen et al., 1979; Kluger & DeNisi, 1996; London & Smither, 2002; Taylor et al., 1984) provide the foundation for most of the concepts discussed in this book. In this brief overview, we have introduced critical components of the feedback process, including the feedback source; feedback message; feedback recipient (including individual differences and the importance of perception); relationship between feedback and goals (e.g., control theory); and the role of context. Each concept is the focus of a subsequent chapter.

We drew on the essential elements of these classic feedback models to develop our own simple model of the feedback process (see Figure 1.5), which highlights four key components of the feedback process: (1) feed-

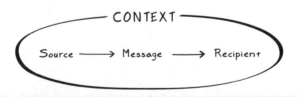

Figure 1.5

Our parsimonious model of the feedback process.

back source, (2) actual feedback message, (3) individual differences of the recipient, and (4) context in which feedback exchanges occur. This model is not intended to replace the models described in this chapter but, rather, to provide a straightforward illustration of the basic building blocks of the feedback process that is useful in professional practice. We reference this model throughout the next several chapters.

This quick overview is heavy on theory and research; with this foundation, we use subsequent chapters to focus more on the application of these concepts and real world examples of how these feedback processes play out in the workplace. We bring each theory and research concept to life with case examples from our four consultants.

2

How Feedback and Goals Drive Behavior: Control Theory

Helen, the executive coach we introduced in the Introduction, is currently working with a client, Connor, who wants to improve his "executive presence." He is hoping to be promoted from director to vice president in the next year. However, Connor has received consistent feedback that he needs to develop his ability to inspire others and to act like a leader. He and his human resources business partner agreed that working with an executive coach could provide Connor with the personalized and high-impact development support he needs.

In the following pages, we discuss Helen and Connor's coaching engagement and, from a control theory perspective, the vital role that feedback plays in that relationship. The Chapter 1 discussion of Taylor, Fisher, and Ilgen (1984) mentioned control theory, which provides an excellent framework for clearly illustrating the value of feedback for helping people understand what they need to do to achieve their goals (see Figure 1.2 for our simple control loop model).

http://dx.doi.org/10.1037/14619-003
Using Feedback in Organizational Consulting, by J. B. Gregory and P. E. Levy

CONTROL THEORY

The basic premise of control theory is that people attempt to regulate their performance on a task by actively monitoring their behavior relative to some standard. This behavioral regulation entails comparing current performance or behavior to a goal or reference point for desired performance. This comparison is enabled by feedback: Individuals gather information about their current level of performance to assess the gap or difference between their current behavior and desired behavior (i.e., the goal or standard). An example most people can relate to is weight management. If someone has a target weight of 150 pounds (the standard or desired state), that person evaluates his or her "performance" by comparing his or her actual weight to that standard. So, when the person receives feedback (in this case, from stepping on the scale) that his or her actual weight has crept up to 155, the individual becomes aware of a gap or discrepancy between his or her current state and the desired state (specifically, a 5-pound gap).

When detecting a gap between current and desired performance, individuals actively alter either their behavior or the goal to reduce the difference between current behavior and the goal state (Carver & Scheier, 1998; Johnson, Chang, & Lord, 2006; Vancouver, 2005). This gap is often referred to as a *goal-performance discrepancy* (GPD), and the desire for discrepancy reduction can be a strong motivator. Responses to a GPD vary widely according to the individual and the situation. Attempts at behavior regulation may include increasing effort, attempting new behaviors or new strategies to target the goal, altering the goal to be less of a stretch, or even abandoning the goal altogether (Campion & Lord, 1982). All of these behaviors can result in a smaller GPD or gap between current and desired performance.

Kluger and DeNisi's (1996) feedback intervention theory (FIT; see Chapter 1) draws heavily on control theory. In FIT, Kluger and DeNisi discussed four strategies individuals can use to eliminate a GPD, which they refer to as a "feedback-standard gap" (p. 259). Similar to the behavior regulation methods presented by Campion and Lord (1982), Kluger and DeNisi noted that, when feedback indicates a discrepancy between current performance and desired performance, individuals can choose to (1) increase effort to alter performance to reduce the discrepancy, (2) abandon the standard, (3) change or revise the standard, or (4) reject the feedback. Let's revisit our weight example in which someone has a goal of weighing 150 pounds and has been taking action to try and achieve this goal by making healthier life choices. When stepping on the scale and weighing in at 160 pounds, the person becomes aware of a discrepancy or gap between a current and desired state. Applying control theory, that individual may act in one of four ways. The person could increase weight loss efforts by eating less and healthier, exercising more, and sleeping more to shrink the GPD by moving the current state closer to the desired one (Response 1: Increase effort to alter performance to reduce the discrepancy). Or, one could simply abandon the goal of decreasing the weight to 150 pounds (Response 2: Abandon the standard). The person could revise the goal to be easier to achieve (Response 3: Change or revise the standard). By adjusting the goal weight to 155 pounds, rather than 150 pounds, the person has reduced the gap between current state (160 pounds) and desired state (155 pounds). The individual can reject the feedback by concluding that the scale is inaccurate and that the weight is less than 160 pounds, so, therefore, a 10-pound gap does not exist between the current and desired states (Response 4: Reject the feedback).

Because it is highlighting a deficit, feedback indicating that one has not achieved one's goal or desired state is considered *negative* feedback. Negative feedback is not synonymous with destructive or harmful feedback—it simply indicates the direction of the discrepancy. Negative feedback tends to be the most useful because it allows people to gauge the distance between where they are and where they want to be, and it frequently provides important insights into how to go about closing that gap. However, individuals are more likely to reject negative feedback than positive feedback (Brett & Atwater, 2001; Ilgen, Fisher, & Taylor, 1979; Kluger & DeNisi, 1996; Nowack & Mashihi, 2012). Chapter 3 provides a more in-depth discussion on the meaning and impact of what is historically referred to as *feedback sign*.

A variety of terms and acronyms are commonly associated with control theory. *Cybernetics* (Wiener, 1948) includes feedback and control processes;

thus, control theory is essentially a cybernetic theory. In 1960, Miller, Galanter, and Pribram used the acronym TOTE to describe the steps involved in a control loop: test, operate, test, exit. The test step involves comparing the current behavior with the standard or goal. The operate step encompasses any follow-up actions used to reduce a detected discrepancy in the test phase. That step is followed by another test to again gauge the discrepancy between current performance and the standard. If the discrepancy has been eliminated and behavior is consistent with the standard, an exit from the control loop follows. The individual has achieved his or her goal, so can move on and focus on another task (perhaps another control loop!). However, in most circumstances, a few iterations of the test-operate-test sequence are necessary to achieve the standard. Thus, the individual may proceed to alter behavior once more and subsequently conduct a test between current behavior and the standard; the person will continue in this loop until achieving the goal.

FEEDBACK IN CONTROL THEORY

Feedback is the fundamental part of the control loop; it provides the critical information that allows individuals to gauge the GPD. In the TOTE model, for instance, some sort of feedback typically informs the test function. Feedback that drives a control loop may be self-generated, come from the environment, or be provided by others. For example, when driving down the highway, one may see a sign indicating a 65-mph speed limit. However, when glancing at the speedometer and noticing that the car is traveling at 73 mph, the feedback from the environment indicates a gap exists between the standard (i.e., going the legal limit of 65 mph) and the current behavior (i.e., going 73 mph). In the context of work, perhaps a coaching client has a goal of being a star at delivering presentations. Because having clear and specific goals makes gauging the GPD easier, the consultant can help the client break an overarching goal into more specific components. For example, what the client really wants to achieve may be having a tone and volume that will keep the audience engaged, connecting with the audience, and ensuring that audience members come away from the presentation with a clear understanding of the topic. When delivering presentations, feedback can be self-generated based on how well a person thinks he or she did in achieving each target. However, feedback from others—audience members, peers, a superior—will provide a more objective perspective. For example, when a colleague provides feedback that a person talks too fast and jumps around erratically from topic to topic, it is easier to gauge the distance between current presentation skills and desired end-state presentation skills. Control loops can be ongoing: The GPD continually shrinks (either because current behavior is getting closer to the goal or because the goal was revised to be less challenging) and ongoing feedback allows the GPD to be regularly assessed.

Control loops are not always so straightforward. Human behavior is complex, and attempts at self-regulation are not always successful. Self-regulatory failures include behaviors like procrastinating, making ineffective behavior changes, persisting too long at a fruitless task, or giving up too soon (Diefendorff & Lord, 2008; Steel, 2007). Consulting psychologists can offer self-regulatory assistance to clients by helping them set smaller, manageable goals that will contribute to their ultimate goal; helping them learn new behaviors and strategies for dealing with self-regulatory challenges (e.g., procrastination); offering encouragement and support as individuals challenge themselves; and providing consistent coaching and feedback as individuals work to reduce GPDs.

Control theory suggests that clients use feedback as valuable information for self-regulation by comparing their current behavior or performance to a standard, such as a goal or desired behavior or performance. In the following section, we illustrate this theory by considering Connor and Helen's executive coaching relationship.

PUTTING IT INTO PRACTICE

Connor's goal is to have better executive presence: to be more effective at inspiring others, which may include better and more energized communication skills; an enhanced ability to connect with others; and an ability to communicate a vision or plans in terms that truly speak to others. Based on a control theory perspective, Connor needs feedback to understand where he currently stands on these criteria: What, exactly, does he need to do to improve his behavior? This initial feedback will help Connor gauge where he currently stands and how far that is from his desired end state. As he had told Helen, his executive coach, he has received feedback that, to be considered for a promotion to vice president, he needs to develop his ability to inspire others and act like a leader. Helen may first want to work with Connor to further flesh out his specific goal. What are specific behaviors he wants to exhibit? How can he break "executive presence" down into more concrete, observable, and targeted behaviors? From a control theory perspective, having a clear and specific standard to work toward will make it easier to give her client constructive feedback and also easier for Connor to target opportunities for behavior change. As Connor starts to further refine his goals, Helen provides him with constructive feedback and helps him understand the value and importance of having clear, specific goals. After several revisions and conversations, Connor and Helen are satisfied with the goals described in Figure 2.1.

GOAL	HOW TO ASSESS?
Use my body language / nonverbal behaviors more effectively to reinforce what I'm trying to accomplish.	Have Helen observe me interacting with others; ask others specifically for feedback about my behavior.
Develop my public speaking skills to have more impact: learn to use tone, deliberate pauses, and eye contact with the audience more effectively.	Videotape a few presentations to see what I'm doing well and where I have room to improve. Try to gauge the level of engagement from the audience when I'm talking.
Generally work on feeling more comfortable in the spotlight. This has traditionally made me very uncomfortable, which comes through in my behavior.	Gauge how I am feeling in situations where I'm in the spotlight; understand that my discomfort may be interpreted by others as being aloof or uninterested; seek to put others at ease.

Figure 2.1

Connor's goals.

Connor's revised goals are now more specific and easier to observe, thereby making it easier for Helen and others to provide feedback that targets desirable behaviors and helps Connor begin to make progress. Now that Connor has clearly articulated his goals (the standard, or referent, in a control loop), he and Helen can work on developing a clear understanding of his current state by measuring his progress toward those goals, thereby allowing an assessment of the GPD. By creating a realistic assessment of his current level of performance through feedback from Helen and others (and his self-generated feedback), Connor can accurately assess his distance from his goal or desired end state. Helen observes Connor in a few one-on-one interactions and also observes him delivering presentations. She provides feedback specific to his goals, focusing on his nonverbal behaviors—his tone, pauses, and eye contact—and on his general behavior when interacting with others.

Although feedback sign is discussed extensively in Chapter 3, note that negative feedback has the most value in a control loop. Control loops are technically negative feedback loops (Carver & Scheier, 1982) because the purpose is to negate or reduce the distance between the current state and desired state. Negative feedback is a challenging topic. On the one hand, it provides the most informational value about what people are doing wrong and what they need to do to improve performance; yet, it is most likely to simultaneously elicit a defensive reaction from the recipient. From a control theory perspective, it is negative feedback that helps individuals gauge the distance between where they are and where they want to be. In Connor's case, when Helen tells him that during his presentation on Tuesday, he failed to make meaningful eye contact with the audience and just read off his notes the entire time, she is not only telling him what he did wrong, she is also helping him to specifically pinpoint behaviors he needs to target if he really wants to improve his performance. When delivered effectively, negative feedback illuminates the distance between the current state and desired state, and can also tell the recipient exactly where he or she needs to focus behavior change to close that discrepancy.

Connor finds Helen's feedback valuable as he works to improve his executive presence. In their next coaching session, they discuss the progress he has made so far. It is clear that Connor is making a concerted effort to better control his behavior (i.e., nonverbal language, tone, eye contact). Helen provides feedback on differences she has noticed in his interactions with individuals and in front of groups; she points out improvements on specific behaviors that Connor has indicated he wants to improve. Connor tells Helen he feels good about his progress. With the additional clarity about where he is compared with where he wants to be, and Helen's clear and specific feedback, Connor feels he has been able to make noticeable progress on his goals: He is developing new skills and behaviors that are improving his communication and executive presence.

The pace of Connor's progress illustrates another important component of control theory: the rate of discrepancy reduction (Carver & Scheier, 1998; Chang, Johnson, & Lord, 2009). When comparing current behavior with a standard, what matters is not just whether the discrepancy is shrinking, but also the rate at which the discrepancy is shrinking. The rate—also referred to as *velocity*—of discrepancy reduction has important implications for affect (i.e., emotion) and continuing motivation. When progress happens quickly (i.e., rapid discrepancy reduction), individuals are more likely to experience positive affect and feel motivated. When progress is slow—particularly if slower than desired or anticipated—the result is typically negative affect and reduced motivation to persist. Furthermore, if progress is going in the opposite direction (e.g., the individual's current performance is moving farther from the standard), the result is also negative affect and lower motivation (Carver & Scheier, 1998; Chang et al., 2009). Slow or no progress tends to result in the individual's having a lower expectation of success.

Control theory can provide a useful framework for thinking about the impact of goal progress on client motivation. When working with individuals, it is critical to be keenly aware of how the client perceives goal progress: whether progress is moving at a desirable rate, faster than expected, or slower than expected. Through years of research, the Corporate Leadership Council (2012b) has found that most performance challenges can be traced to one of these root causes: lack of skill, unclear expectations, external barriers, or lack of motivation. When addressing performance challenges, it is imperative to target the right root cause, and understanding if progress toward goals is playing a role in motivation will be critical to this analysis. Consultants may need to help clients work through barriers and challenges that are preventing the desired level of goal progress and attainment.

The impact of goal progress on motivation also has important implications for Helen and Connor's work. For example, if Helen and Connor only schedule coaching sessions once a month, Connor may have to wait up to 4 weeks to get additional feedback on his behavior and progress from Helen. In a situation like Connor's in which he is motivated and dedicated to making changes to behaviors that are challenging and a little uncomfortable for him, waiting too long for feedback that will help him gauge progress has noticeable implications for his emotions and motivation. Helen has noticed that Connor experiences a great deal of positive emotion when he feels he's making progress toward his goal, which further motivates him. To ensure that he is receiving sufficient feedback to help him gauge his progress, Helen suggests that Connor try to get feedback from peers, colleagues, and even friends and family members. Connor has never been comfortable with actively seeking out feedback, but Helen encourages him to go outside of his comfort zone to gain additional insights. She believes that getting regular feedback that indicates progress in the right direction—even if only in small increments—will help Connor remain positive and motivated to pursue his goals. Helen pushes Connor to identify strategies for staying focused on his goals and to continue to work on building his skills when he runs into challenges or feels discouraged.

Over the course of the next 4 months, and with the help of feedback from Helen and an array of trusted colleagues and companions, Connor shows improvements in his self-awareness around his executive presence and works hard to target the specific goals and behaviors he set out to achieve. Although he has a ways to go, Connor becomes more adept at gauging his own behavior and the impact that it has on others. He feels he has reduced the distance between where he was several months ago and where he wants to be. Connor knows that achieving this goal will require continued effort and persistence, but he has come to see feedback—self-generated and from others—as a critical source of information to help him gauge his GPD. In addition, in discovering just how valuable feedback can be for understanding his behavior, Connor has begun to overcome his discomfort with actively seeking out feedback from others—a topic that is discussed in Chapter 5.

CONCLUSION

Control theory is a useful framework for thinking about how goals and feedback are inherently linked. Control theory lends itself to an array of examples and analogies that can be useful in a consulting practice. Clients who are engineers, for example, will likely understand the thermostat comparison,[1] which can help explain human behavior and motivation in terms they can appreciate. Coaches and consulting psychologists may find control theory valuable in helping them think about where their clients currently stand compared to where those clients want to be. Getting a sense for this discrepancy can help coaches or consultants to be intentional in the feedback they provide to clients to help them stay motivated, stay positive, and have greater clarity about what needs to change for goal achievement.

Next, we take a more in-depth look at the actual feedback message and how nuances in feedback statements contribute to how feedback recipients perceive the message.

---

[1]A thermostat operates as a cybernetic control loop; it compares the current room temperature with the set, or desired, temperature and acts by producing heat or cool air to reduce any discrepancy. For instance, if a thermostat is set at 68 (the standard), but in the depths of winter the room temperature falls to 62, the thermostat will detect a discrepancy between the current room temperature and the standard, and will produce heat to reduce that discrepancy. Drawing on the TOTE example, after operating (i.e., producing heat), another test is conducted to reassess the discrepancy. Once the current temperature matches the set temperature and the discrepancy is eliminated, an exit from the control loop occurs: The furnace stops producing hot air.

3

Getting to the Point: The Feedback Message

Our review of classic models of the feedback process (Ilgen, Fisher, & Taylor, 1979; Kluger & DeNisi, 1996; London & Smither, 2002; Taylor, Fisher, & Ilgen, 1984) in Chapter 1 highlighted a number of factors that impact how individuals perceive, interpret, and respond to feedback. One factor is the content and form of the message itself. Regardless of who is giving the feedback or how open to or avoidant of feedback the recipient is, aspects of the actual feedback message will play an important role in how he or she receives and interprets that message, and whether the recipient will actually do anything with it.

In this chapter, we focus on nuances of the feedback message that affect how effectively or ineffectively it resonates with the recipient. These critical ingredients include the sign of the feedback (positive vs. negative), the type of feedback (e.g., outcome vs. process feedback), and the focus of the feedback (e.g., on the person's character or personality vs. his or her

http://dx.doi.org/10.1037/14619-004
Using Feedback in Organizational Consulting, by J. B. Gregory and P. E. Levy

behavior). Many of these factors are also influenced by the way in which feedback is delivered—the focus of Chapter 4.

FEEDBACK SIGN

One of the most common ways to categorize feedback is according to its *sign* or *valence*, that is, whether feedback is positive or negative. Ilgen et al. (1979) highlighted feedback sign as one of the three vital elements that impact the recipient's desire to respond to feedback. It is important to make the distinction between negative feedback and destructive feedback (London, 2003). Both positive and negative feedback can be constructive or destructive—that is, delivered and worded in a way that either helps or harms the recipient, respectively. Constructive feedback provides the recipient with useful and specific information that is not hurtful to the recipient (R. A. Baron, 1988; London, 2003). It is easy to make the incorrect assumption that negative feedback is hurtful, inaccurate, or downright mean, or that it furthers an ulterior motive. However, the term *negative* simply refers to the performance deficit (e.g., the gap between actual and desired performance, such as the goal performance discrepancy [GPD] discussed in Chapter 2) that is observed and described through the feedback. Positive feedback, in contrast, indicates that behavior is meeting or exceeding expectations. In lay terms, positive and negative feedback are synonymous with praise and constructive criticism, respectively.

Positive and negative feedback can be formal or informal, broad or specific, or focused on ongoing work or final evaluations (also referred to as *process and outcome feedback*, which is described later in this chapter). Examples of positive feedback may include something as simple as saying "great job on that presentation" or "your performance this year was right on track" to more specific comments, such as "the language that you used to explain complex financial modeling in the quarterly report was perfect; the straightforward way that you wrote it will help people without a finance background understand what we are trying to achieve." Similarly, negative feedback can be broad and general, such as in an unsatisfactory performance rating that loosely addresses where the employee failed to meet expectations throughout the year. Negative feedback can also be specific and targeted at precisely what someone needs to do to improve. For example, telling a direct report that a presentation "would have been stronger if there had been less text on the slides" and if the person had "spoken louder and made eye contact with the audience" helps the employee to identify exactly what he or she can do differently to have a stronger presentation next time.

The discussion of control theory in Chapter 2 touched on the role of feedback sign in assessing the GPD. Kluger and DeNisi (1996) drew on control theory and also emphasized the role of feedback sign in their feedback intervention theory (FIT). A core argument of FIT is that feedback sign results from a comparison of current performance to the standard or desired outcome. This comparison will always result in either positive (i.e., goal is achieved) or negative (a gap still exists between current performance and the goal state) feedback. Based on this control theory perspective, negative feedback is the most useful because it offers information about how far someone is from achieving the standard or desired state. Positive feedback is also useful, but it does not provide information about where GPDs exist and, therefore, where one needs to focus resources.

Herein lies the great paradox of negative feedback: It is the most useful form of feedback, yet it is the form that people like the least. Furthermore, people are more likely to reject or dismiss negative feedback (Brett & Atwater, 2001; Ilgen et al., 1979; Kluger & DeNisi, 1996; Nowack & Mashihi, 2012). Although negative feedback may have greater informational value, people generally tend to like positive feedback better and are more likely to respond more favorably to it (London, 2003). Research has consistently demonstrated that people tend to have inflated self-views that may lead to disagreement between their perceptions of their own behavior and feedback provided by others (Ashford & Tsui, 1991; Atwater & Brett, 2005; Vecchio & Anderson, 2009). Numerous studies have documented the ubiquity of the *above average effect*: people's tendency to hold self-enhancing beliefs and rate themselves as above average on everything from driving (Guerin, 1994; McKenna & Myers, 1997), to physical attractiveness (Epley & Whitchurch, 2008), to their competence at work (Gawande, 2002; Headey & Wearing,

1988). These inflated self-views, or positive illusions, are not necessarily a bad thing, because they can help protect against depression and promote well-being (Taylor & Brown, 1988). However, having these inflated self-views can make people less open to accurate, constructive negative feedback because it fails to confirm what we think about ourselves. Thus, negative feedback may elicit a strong emotional response, defensiveness, and rejection of the feedback (Ashford & Tsui, 1991; Ilgen et al., 1979; London, 2003). In addition to self-views, a number of other individual differences influence how people react and respond to negative feedback (Linderbaum & Levy, 2010; Raftery & Bizer, 2009; Robinson, Moeller, & Fetterman, 2010). These individual differences, which include regulatory focus, feedback orientation, and personality variables such as neuroticism and openness, among others, are discussed at length in Chapter 5.

Although negative feedback has informational value for helping the recipient understand the gap between performance and the standard—and what might need to happen to close that gap—positive feedback also has a great deal of value, and people generally like positive feedback (London, 2003). It reaffirms that they are performing well and reinforces their behaviors. It lets them know that their efforts have not been for naught and that their effort and persistence have resulted in positive outcomes.

Self-efficacy theorists, such as Albert Bandura (1986), have argued that positive feedback builds self-efficacy, reinforces behavior, and results in higher levels of subsequent performance. *Self-efficacy* is an individual's belief that he or she has the skills and capability necessary to complete a particular task (Bandura, 1986). However, other researchers have noted that positive feedback can also result in reduced effort or motivation (Campion & Lord, 1982; Cianci, Schaubroeck, & McGill, 2010; Walker & Smither, 1999). Some researchers (Fishbach, Eyal, & Finkelstein, 2010; Weick, 1984) have suggested that failure, rather than success, is more of a motivator. Returning to control theory, discerning a substantial gap between current state and desired state can motivate individuals to accelerate their performance and increase effort. On the contrary, once individuals have achieved the goal or standard, they may be less inclined to put forth the same level of effort that results in performance that got them to their goal; therefore, they may slack off on subsequent behavior.

Overall, the effect of positive and negative feedback on performance is not entirely straightforward. Other factors play a role in the effect of both positive and negative feedback on recipient reactions and behavior. Feedback delivery and individual differences of the recipient, which can interact with the feedback message to affect outcomes, are discussed in Chapters 4 and 5, respectively. For example, the way in which negative feedback is delivered and the credibility of the feedback source affect recipient perceptions of negative feedback (Steelman & Rutkowski, 2004). In addition, individuals who have a favorable feedback orientation (i.e., they value, seek, and use feedback) may be more open to and appreciative of constructive negative feedback than a colleague with a less favorable feedback orientation (Linderbaum & Levy, 2010). However, other aspects of the actual feedback message also impact the effects of positive and negative feedback on recipient reactions and behaviors. One such aspect is the type of feedback.

FEEDBACK TYPE

Feedback can be general or specific, and it can address ongoing work or provide a final evaluation of someone's work or behavior. Not only is the recipient more likely to accept specific feedback, such feedback is more likely to help that recipient understand exactly what he or she needs to change or do differently to improve performance. Specific negative feedback allows the recipient to understand exactly what aspect of performance did not meet expectations, whereas specific positive feedback helps the recipient understand exactly what is was that he or she did well, thus increasing the likelihood that the person will repeat that good behavior. Specific feedback is also more easily applied to behavior change because it pinpoints the very behaviors that need to be changed. People are more likely to learn from specific, as opposed to general, feedback, because it helps them understand precisely what they are doing well or poorly and why it matters (Ilgen et al., 1979; Shute, 2008; Strijbos, Narciss, & Dünnebier, 2010). Consultants should not only strive to provide the most specific feedback possible to clients to increase self-awareness and drive behavior change, but also help clients build their own feedback skills by seeking to provide the most specific feedback possible to their direct reports, peers, and coworkers. One strategy to consider is to encourage clients to ask themselves, "Can I be more specific in this feedback?" before providing it to others, or to think about how clearly the recipient will be able to pinpoint the specific action that they executed well or poorly.

Another way to conceptualize feedback is as either process or outcome feedback, a distinction introduced by Earley, Northcraft, Lee, and Lituchy (1990). *Process feedback* provides information about the way in which something is done, whereas *outcome feedback* focuses on an overall evaluation of the results (Earley et al., 1990; Medvedeff, Gregory, & Levy, 2008). For example, in organizations, providing employees with regular, informal feedback about how they are getting their work done could be categorized as process feedback, whereas their annual performance evaluation score is outcome feedback. Outcome feedback is inherently evaluation oriented (Medvedeff et al., 2008) and provides little information that recipients can use to change behavior. Outcome feedback provides an assessment of someone's performance and generally comes after completion of the task, thus not providing the individual an opportunity to change behavior. This is one of the many reasons why employees generally tend to dislike the annual performance evaluation process; it leaves them feeling judged and evaluated, and with little opportunity to take action on critical feedback they receive. It is comparable to a final grade in an academic course. On the other hand, process feedback provides recipients with real-time feedback on what they are doing well or poorly as they work toward a result or end state. Because it is in process, individuals have the opportunity to use the feedback to change their behavior or course correct to ensure a desirable outcome.

Crossing feedback type with feedback sign results in different reactions and behaviors from feedback recipients. Medvedeff et al. (2008) suggested that the two most desirable combinations for acting on feedback and motivating behavior change are negative process feedback and positive outcome feedback (see Figure 3.1 for an illustration of this interaction). These authors found that individuals were most likely to seek additional feedback when they received negative process feedback that

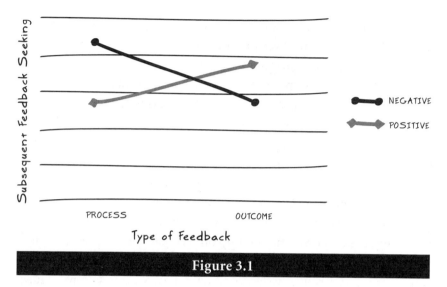

Figure 3.1

The interactive effect of feedback sign and type on subsequent feedback seeking.

told them what they were doing wrong and what they could improve to have better performance as they worked through a task. Receiving positive outcome feedback also drove high levels of subsequent feedback seeking, although not as much as negative process feedback did. Based on a self-efficacy or reinforcement perspective, individuals may have sought more feedback simply because they appreciated knowing that they were doing a good job and enjoyed the praise and reinforcement. Interestingly, individuals who received only negative outcome feedback were less likely to seek additional feedback. By only receiving negative outcome feedback, individuals were not provided with helpful, directional guidance about what they could be doing better. Instead, they were only told that their performance was poor. The negative outcome feedback did not indicate what aspects of performance were poor or provide any insights into the nature of the problem, which presumably demotivated participants in subsequent trials. Positive outcome feedback was rewarding, and negative process feedback provided useful information to help individuals improve; thus, these particular combinations were most motivating, but for different reasons.

Receiving only negative outcome feedback, despite attempts at behavior modification and improved performance, could easily result in learned helplessness. *Learned helplessness* is a phenomenon in which an individual attempts to change poor performance or a negative situation, but, despite all attempts, sees no improvement, which signals to the individual that he or she has little to no control over the situation (Seligman, 1975). As a result, individuals may simply give up and cease any additional attempts to change their behavior or the situation. For example, say an employee consistently receives negative outcome feedback devoid of process feedback from her manager. Despite active attempts at performance improvement, the employee continues to receive only negative outcome feedback. Eventually, the employee may give up on trying to improve performance because no connection seems to exist between attempts at behavior change and the manager's evaluative feedback. Self-efficacy theorists have argued that positive feedback in response to even small improvements in performance is imperative to keeping individuals motivated in their pursuit of behavior change.

In organizational contexts, the majority of critical feedback events are the direct manager's responsibility. Organizational consultants—internal to organizations or hired as external consultants—need to be aware of the critical role of managers in providing feedback to staff and need to make efforts to educate managers on the distinction between outcome and process feedback, and how each can impact performance and motivation. In the current authors' experience with training managers on key feedback skills, distinguishing between these two types of feedback and the impact they can have on performance is eye-opening for managers, most of whom recognize the importance of feedback but are often unaware of the distinctions.

FOCUS OF THE FEEDBACK MESSAGE

The focus of the feedback message has important implications for how recipients will react to positive and negative feedback. When providing an individual with feedback—positive or negative—that feedback can focus either on the individual's actions and behavior or on the individual as a person, such as his or her personality, character, or abilities. As a rule of thumb, feedback should always focus on behavior, not on the individual as a person. If the ultimate goal of feedback is to drive behavior change, then feedback needs to focus on behaviors. Consulting psychologists should be the first to acknowledge that it is much easier for a person to change his or her behavior than to change who he or she is as a person.

If that is not enough to convince you, research has consistently demonstrated that negative feedback—which indicates that performance is not meeting expectations or current behavior is not aligned with desired behavior—is most effective when it focuses on an individual's actions or behavior (Kluger & DeNisi, 1996; London, 2003; O'Malley & Gregory, 2011; Whetten & Cameron, 2002). For instance, Kluger and DeNisi (1996) found that feedback that threatened recipients' self-esteem because it was critical of their intelligence or them as a person was significantly less likely to have a positive effect on performance. Behavior- or task-focused feedback is more conducive to action than person-focused feedback; people are more likely to accept and respond favorably to negative feedback when they feel they have some control over the actions in question (Larson, 1984; London, 2003).

Person-focused feedback is counterproductive for several reasons. It is far less likely to result in change, because changing one's abilities or who one is as a person is challenging—much more so than changing specific actions or behaviors. Feedback that targets the individual as a person directs attention inward, toward the self, rather than toward the task. Providing feedback on characteristics, such as personality, can pose challenges for the feedback recipient. For example, telling clients that they may struggle with relationship building at work because they are very introverted may leave them feeling as if their natural inclinations make them insufficient and unclear about what follow-up actions to take. A better alternative would be to focus the feedback on specific behaviors, which may align to introversion/extraversion but are not as seemingly immutable as personality traits. Behavior or task-focused feedback directs the feedback recipient's attention to the task, rather than activates unnecessary and distracting self-consciousness and self-focus. In addition, negative person-focused feedback may result in the recipient's feeling defensive, hurt, and likely to dismiss or reject the feedback. For example, characterizing someone as being a bad writer sends a very different message than stating that significant revisions to a report are needed.

When it comes to positive feedback, however, some researchers have disagreed about where feedback should focus. For example, London (2003) suggested that constructive feedback attributes strong performance to either effort or ability. However, other researchers have demonstrated that praising one's ability rather than effort can have negative consequences. Over the course of six different studies, Mueller and Dweck (1998) demonstrated that individuals praised for their abilities were more likely to focus on performance, as opposed to learning, and show less persistence and less enjoyment of a task than those who were praised for their hard work. Through her stream of research, Dweck (2006) demonstrated that children who were praised for their efforts and hard work rather than their abilities were more likely to persist in the face of failure. When individuals were praised for their abilities, they attributed their successes to those abilities, rather than to their work or effort. As a result, when those individuals failed, they automatically attributed the failure to their insufficient abilities. In attributing their failures to a lack of abilities, those individuals may have given up on the task at hand because they believed they were incapable of succeeding. On the basis of that research, best practice indicates that, whenever possible, both positive and negative feedback should focus on controllable actions and behaviors exhibited by clients.

Positive feedback should focus on an individual's hard work and efforts, rather than her or his inherent abilities. Even praise that addresses an aspect of a person's character and personality can be phrased to focus on behavior. For example, rather than telling a client, "Michael, I think you are a really high-integrity person," that feedback could be reframed to say, "Michael, you demonstrated a lot of integrity when you admitted your mistakes to your team this afternoon. I was really impressed." In this example, if Michael were to have a moral failing in the future, he would not have to revise his self-concept to be less high-integrity; instead, he could explain that moral failing by focusing on his specific actions and behaviors in that specific instance.

Both positive and negative feedback have a great deal of value, but the type of feedback, level of specificity, and focus of the feedback also play critical roles. In the next section, we consider how these aspects of the feedback message can be incorporated into practice.

PUTTING IT INTO PRACTICE

In the Introduction to this volume, we introduced Lane, a consulting psychologist who works as an internal consultant for a global Fortune 100 organization. Lane designs processes and tools that are used by human resources (HR) business partners throughout the business. Currently, she is working on redesigning the company's internal 360° feedback tool. A *360°* or *multisource feedback instrument* is one in which feedback about a specific individual is solicited (generally via an online assessment tool) from a variety of colleagues, including supervisors, direct reports, peers, and other business partners. As a result, participants get a holistic, 360-degree look at how they are perceived by others with whom they work closely. Feedback is generally anonymous but often grouped by category (i.e., peers, clients, direct reports). This tool has been popular with HR, line managers, and individual employees because it provides an extensive feedback report with perspectives from a variety of colleagues. Individual employees can initiate a 360° assessment anytime they want, and include up to 15 raters, such as their manager, peers, direct reports, other associates throughout the organization (e.g., key partners in other functions), and even individuals outside of the organization, such as clients or outside vendor partners. Despite the tool's popularity, Lane has received feedback that people sometimes have difficulty knowing what to do with the feedback they have received. Turning that feedback into development intentions and actions has posed a challenge for many employees throughout the organization. Therefore, Lane has decided it is time to revisit the 360° feedback report. She plans to draw on best practices in crafting feedback messages to create a new report that is even more valuable and actionable than the existing one.

Lane takes time to review the current report and, to get additional feedback on how the report could be improved, conducts a few focus groups with individuals who have used the report. In drawing on her knowledge of feedback research and best practices, she realizes that the feedback provided by the report tends to be focused on the person (i.e., a person's abilities rather than efforts), and the feedback messages are somewhat general and vague. Using a 5-point scale ranging from 1 *(development opportunity)* to 5 *(key strength)*, the 360° tool asks raters to assess the target individual on behaviors aligned with 16 key competencies. In addition, all of the open-ended questions for which raters can provide written feedback are written to elicit outcome rather than process feedback.

By integrating her knowledge of the 360° feedback report with ideas for best practices that she gleaned from the feedback literature, Lane identifies several key revisions that she thinks will result in a better 360° feedback report—one that will better drive participant follow-up and development action. First, she revises the feedback messages generated to match the scores associated with each competency. She plugs a different prewritten feedback message into the report based on the individual's numeric rating on each competency. So, for each of the 16 competencies, employees will receive both numerical ratings and a feedback message explaining that rating in more detail. Lane revises all statements to be less focused on abilities and more focused on actions and behaviors so that, when individuals read their reports, they will have better success translating the feedback into development goals, because it focuses on behaviors, rather than abilities.

While revising the feedback statements, Lane notes that the existing statements are not very specific. They provide vague, general statements about the overarching competency. To improve the feedback statements, Lane digs into the specific items that comprise the assessment to see exactly which behaviors are included with each competency. She revises the feedback statements to address each specific behavior rated in the assessment. As a result, the feedback statements are more precise and correspond to more specific behaviors rather than high-level, overarching competencies. In addition, to provide employees a jump start in turning feedback into development goals, she builds into the report a few developmental recommendations for each feedback message. As a result, the feedback message not only identifies for employees what they were perceived as doing well or poorly, but also suggests follow-up actions they can take.

Next, Lane revises the open-ended comment questions that raters had the option of answering. She had already discovered that these questions elicited outcome-focused feedback from the raters. Lane recognizes that some outcome feedback can be useful, specifically when it is positive outcome feedback. Thus, Lane leaves one question in at the end of the assessment that asks raters to list final positive comments about the employee's performance and areas of strength. Lane believes that ending the report with this overall, positive evaluative feedback will leave employees with a confidence boost and build their self-efficacy to pursue behavior change, even if much of the report is negative.

Pleased with the revised feedback statements, Lane decides on a few changes to the 360° report to make it even more user-friendly and development oriented. Because of the organization's size, Lane will not be able to debrief everyone who completes the 360° report to help them work through it. As an alternative, she adds sections and writes throughout the report in a tone that mimics a coaching voice-over to help participants work through the report like they would with a coach or facilitator. Based on her review of the feedback literature and input from employee focus groups, Lane knows that people tend to have strong emotional reactions to negative feedback they receive in their report. She believes that if people could reframe the way they think about negative feedback, they might be able to get more value out of the report. Therefore, she adds a new section to the beginning of the 360° feedback report that equips employees who receive 360° feedback with new knowledge about getting the most out of negative feedback.

In this new section Lane adds several piece of caution and advice for users, such as the following:

- People tend to have an initial emotional reaction to negative feedback, so be sure to allow yourself sufficient time to mindfully process and think about the negative feedback.
- Try not to become preoccupied with your emotional reaction and dismiss feedback that you either disagree with or do not like. Instead,

come back and review the feedback later—after your initial emotional reaction has subsided and you can think about it more objectively.

■ When you receive negative feedback or feedback that you don't agree with, try to think of specific examples or situations in which you have exhibited a particular behavior. Try to pinpoint if that behavior only happens in select situations or under certain circumstances.

Following the launch a few months later of the updated 360° feedback report, Lane implements a follow-up survey and conducts a few focus groups with early recipients of the new report to learn how people reacted to the report and how they were using it. She learns that people found value in the educational component at the beginning of the report. Several employees tell her they valued learning more about normal reactions to negative feedback and how slowing down and thinking deeply could make negative feedback a useful resource. Although Lane did receive critical comments and pushback on changes to the report, employees and managers alike generally indicated that the specific and development-focused feedback messages were more conducive to making follow-up development plans. The process-oriented comments from raters translate easily to behavior change, but the overall positive evaluation comments at the end of the report leave employees feeling good about their ability to persist and pursue development. Lane recognizes that the assessment and report will require regular maintenance and updating, but believes that these latest changes have helped refocus the assessment on what really matters: gaining new self-insights and driving behavior change.

CONCLUSION

These critical characteristics of the feedback message—sign, type, specificity, focus—have significant implications for how feedback is accepted and whether it will lead to follow-up actions and behavior change. Above and beyond the actual message, the way that feedback is delivered also impacts how recipients are likely to react to feedback. In the preceding example, characteristics of effective feedback were leveraged to produce higher-quality automated feedback. These nuances are important for using feedback in a consulting practice for a number of reasons. First and foremost, consultants should adhere to these best practices when delivering feedback to their own clients. They should also seek to educate clients—whether individuals or groups within organizations—on these key characteristics of effective feedback and how they impact recipient reactions and subsequent behavior. Of particular importance are recognizing the value of negative feedback and ensuring that feedback focuses on behaviors, not the individual as a person. We encourage all consultants to similarly recognize the criticality of these two points.

In the next two chapters, we shift our focus to characteristics and behaviors of the feedback provider and how they can impact the feedback exchange. In addition, we look at how the recipient's individual differences, past experiences, and characteristics play a vital role in the feedback process.

4

Feedback Delivery and the Role of the Feedback Provider

As discussed in Chapter 3, the actual content of a feedback message influences the recipient's interpretation of and reaction to that feedback. In addition to the message content, the way in which the feedback message is delivered also has important implications for the recipient's perceptions of the feedback—whether or not the feedback is accepted—and subsequent behavior (e.g., motivation, performance). In this chapter, we focus on feedback delivery, including the who (e.g., the feedback source) and the how (e.g., the medium, timing, frequency) of feedback delivery. Although feedback can come from a variety of sources (e.g., task, self, others), the focus of this chapter is on feedback provided by others.

http://dx.doi.org/10.1037/14619-005
Using Feedback in Organizational Consulting, by J. B. Gregory and P. E. Levy

THE FEEDBACK SOURCE

Returning to our simple model (see Figure 1.5), we see that the feedback source is one of the four critical components of the feedback process. The feedback source provides the feedback, and the source's actions and behaviors have a significant impact on how the recipient will receive the feedback. In a consulting context, understanding the role of the feedback source is imperative for several reasons. First and foremost, organizational consultants may often find themselves in the position of feedback source—providing a client with observations about his or her behavior, sharing assessment results, or providing honest feedback and reflection in a coaching context. Consultants may also coach or consult with others who are feedback sources, whether high-level leaders or frontline managers responsible for providing feedback to direct reports, human resources (HR) professionals preparing to provide feedback to business leaders in a strategic planning retreat, or staff who are expected to deliver feedback to peers and colleagues in a team-building exercise. Clients who receive feedback will also benefit from learning more about the role of the feedback source to help them parse elements of the feedback message (e.g., separate emotional reactions to the message versus emotional reactions to how or by whom it was delivered).

In their seminal paper on the feedback process, Ilgen, Fisher, and Taylor (1979) noted that it is difficult to separate the effect of the feedback message from the effect of the feedback source. The source is the face of the feedback and therefore is inherently entangled with the recipient's perception and experience of the feedback event. Ilgen et al. suggested that the feedback source may be the most important factor in whether the recipient accepts the feedback. The attribute that Ilgen et al. emphasized in their work was the source's credibility.

Source Credibility

Credibility can be defined in several ways. Ilgen et al. (1979) described credibility as consisting of the source's level of expertise and trustworthiness. Expertise pertains to the source's ability to accurately judge and assess the recipient's behavior; it includes the source's familiarity with the task at hand and with the individual's performance. In addition to possessing the necessary expertise, the source must also be considered trustworthy by the feedback recipient to be considered credible. The recipient must trust the feedback source's motives and believe that he or she has good intentions in providing the feedback. Ilgen et al. suggested that feedback is more readily accepted when the recipient trusts the source.

Ultimately, source credibility impacts the recipient's perception of the feedback message. Recipients are more likely to rate the feedback message and the feedback source more favorably when they believe the source to be credible (Albright & Levy, 1995). Feedback is also more likely to be perceived as accurate when it comes from a credible source (Ilgen et al., 1979; Stone, Guetal, & McIntosh, 1984; Taylor, Fisher, & Ilgen, 1984). Even with upward feedback (e.g., feedback given from a subordinate to a superior), source expertise increases the likelihood that constructive feedback will result in higher subsequent performance (Tuckman & Oliver, 1968). For instance, if an employee provides feedback to his or her manager, that feedback is more likely to result in behavior change if the manager believes that the employee is trustworthy and knows what he or she is talking about (e.g., possesses expertise). In addition, not only are people more accepting of feedback provided by a credible source, they are also more likely to proactively seek feedback from sources they believe possess expertise (Vancouver & Morrison, 1995). People value the perspectives of individuals they believe are knowledgeable and who have their best intentions at heart.

The Importance of Relationships

Researchers have investigated a number of other attributes of the source that play an important role in feedback exchanges. Several authors have discussed the importance of trustworthiness (Ilgen et al., 1979; Taylor et al., 1984), a key ingredient in another aspect of the feedback exchange: the relationship between the feedback source and feedback recipient. High-quality relationships and supportiveness have been linked to increased feedback-seeking behavior (Vancouver & Morrison, 1995; Williams, Miller, Steelman, & Levy, 1999). On the other hand, low-quality relationships between the source and feedback recipient can lead to feedback avoidance behavior by some recipients (Moss, Sanchez, Brumbaugh, & Borkowski, 2009). When the feedback source and recipient have a poor relationship, recipients may actively avoid the source and the feedback the source may provide. Subsequently, that feedback avoidance behavior may result in poor performance. Moss and Sanchez (2004) suggested that employees may be more inclined to actively avoid getting feedback from managers who are intolerant of failure, psychologically distant, or regularly look for faults in others—those who are not perceived as trustworthy or credible.

In addition, Sparr and Sonnentag (2008) found that relationship quality was related to the perceived fairness of feedback, which also predicted the recipient's self-reported job satisfaction, feelings of control at work, and turnover intentions (negatively related; employees with higher feelings of fairness had lower turnover intentions). When a manager and employee have a high-quality relationship, that employee is more likely to feel that the manager's feedback is fair and, therefore, is more likely to feel satisfied with the job, feel in control of his or her work, and be more likely to stay in that job or with the organization. Similarly favorable interpersonal relationships between the source and the feedback recipient can lead to more positive perceptions of feedback and subsequently higher levels of intrinsic motivation (Pat-El, Tillema, & van Koppen, 2012). Supportive manager behavior during formal feedback events, such as performance appraisals, impacts not only the recipient's motivation to improve, but also his or her actual subsequent performance (Burke, Weitzel, & Weir, 1978; Nemeroff & Wexley, 1979; Sorenson & Franks, 1972; Taylor et al., 1984). Burke et al. (1978) also found that when the feedback source goes beyond simply delivering feedback to discussing with the recipient how he or she could go about improving performance, the recipient indicated a higher level of motivation to improve.

Leadership Style

A leadership style that is focused on caring about individual needs and development enables better feedback exchanges. Employees are more likely to actively seek feedback from leaders who use a transformational style (Levy, Cober, & Miller, 2002) that emphasizes person-centered, development-oriented interactions with followers. Individuals are likely to seek even more feedback from leaders who use individual consideration, that is, leaders who are concerned with each employee's unique needs, interests, and capabilities. The results of a study by Levy et al. (2002) suggested that a leader's use of individual consideration resulted in followers who intended to seek more feedback. Contrast that style with a transactional leadership style in which leaders provide contingent rewards in exchange for staff's completing assigned tasks (Bass, 1985) or leaders who practice management by exception (i.e., intervening only when things go wrong; otherwise, they are hands-off). Such leaders tend to provide feedback to employees only when those employees make mistakes, and relationships are not actively cultivated. Indeed, some individuals would prefer not to provide feedback at all, regardless of whether it is positive or negative (Hillman, Schwandt, & Bartz, 1990). Although they may not realize it, managers and leaders create a culture through their use of, and expectations for, feedback, which, in turn, impacts employee feedback behavior and norms (London & Smither, 2002; Steelman, Levy, & Snell, 2004). This notion of a feedback environment is discussed in Chapter 6.

Overall, supportiveness and a certain level of psychological closeness (Ilgen et al., 1979; Moss & Sanchez, 2004; Van den Bossche, Segers, & Jansen, 2010) from the source can enhance the recipient's feedback experience. Using a social network analysis approach, Van den Bossche et al. found that feedback from close social ties resulted in higher performance than feedback from sources with whom the recipient had weak relationships. However, there can be too much of a good thing: Individuals who are overly supportive may seek to avoid giving negative feedback, perhaps because they fear hurting the other person's feelings or they may be uncomfortable dealing with the recipient's emotional reactions (Moss & Sanchez, 2004). Indeed, many managers would agree that giving negative feedback is an unpleasant experience. Moss and Sanchez (2004) suggested that overly supportive feedback sources can become more comfortable delivering negative feedback by reframing the way they think about it. One alternative way to think about negative feedback is as a valuable diagnostic—that is, it provides specific information about an individual's opportunity areas and about ways to improve in those problem areas. By recognizing the developmental value of negative feedback, coming from the perspective of a learning mindset, and even scripting the feedback ahead of time, conflict-avoidant or overly nurturing sources can become more comfortable delivering negative feedback, which, in many ways, is the most important and potentially useful feedback for recipients. Think about the types of feedback you received in the past week: When receiving positive feedback, it may have felt good, but did it make you more effective? If you received negative feedback in the past week, did you have an immediate emotional reaction? It may have been more challenging to accept, but it probably provided useful information that could be used to improve performance if that feedback was delivered well, and by a credible and trusted source.

Power and Status

Another attribute of the source that can affect a feedback exchange is the source's status or power over the feedback recipient. Ilgen et al. (1979) noted that feedback is more likely to be perceived as accurate if the source has substantial power over the recipient. The feedback recipient will also be more likely to respond to and act on the feedback when the source has status, power, or influence. Fedor, Davis, Maslyn, and Mathieson (2001) noted that Ilgen et al. considered only one type of power: that in which the recipient is expected to comply with the source. Fedor et al. drew on French and Raven's (1959) multidimensional concept of power to determine if certain types of power exerted more influence in a feedback exchange. French and Raven had identified five types of power: (1) legitimate power (power derived from holding a formal position); (2) reward power (power derived from having control over resources or rewards that others want); (3) referent power (power derived from seeming attractive or having the ability to command others' interest and respect); (4) expert power (power derived from having critical skills or expertise); and (5) coercive power (power derived from the ability to punish others). Fedor et al. found that negative feedback from sources with either expert (the source is considered to possess expertise) or referent (the source is looked on as a role model, is admired by the recipient) power was more likely to lead to improved performance. This was not the case for coercive power (the source can force the recipient to comply). Similarly, Vancouver and Morrison (1995) examined another type of power: reward power. They found that individuals are more likely to seek feedback from a source that has power and control over rewards, a finding that has been demonstrated consistently in the literature (Ashford & Tsui, 1991; Morrison & Bies, 1991; Northcraft & Ashford, 1990).

When no power differential exists between the feedback source and recipient (e.g., peer-to-peer feedback), negative feedback is more likely to result in a negative emotional reaction (Strijbos, Narciss, & Dünnebier, 2010). However, when the feedback recipient believes that his or her peer feedback provider is competent, the recipient tends to view feedback more favorably than when perceiving the peer as being incompetent (Strijbos et al., 2010). Research has also demonstrated that the nature of a peer relationship (e.g., a closer relationship, the importance of the issue at hand, expectations for the recipient's behavior) determines whether a source will provide or withhold negative feedback from a peer (Lundgren & Rudawsky, 2000). Individuals are also more likely to actively seek feedback from superiors, as opposed to peers, presumably because superiors possess the power, influence, and access to desirable resources that peers may lack (Ashford, Blatt, & VandeWalle, 2003; Ashford & Tsui, 1991). The dynamics of the feedback exchange are different in peer relationships than in hierarchical relationships in which a power differential usually exists. Consultants should recognize the influence of this power differential in working with clients and be mindful that feedback exchanges with peers may be perceived differently than those with superiors.

The credibility—including the expertise and trustworthiness—of a feedback source and his or her relationship with the feedback recipient, and the source's level of support, leadership style, and power or status all affect the recipient's acceptance of, reaction to, and likelihood of using the feedback. However, the source alone is not the only important aspect of feedback delivery: The how of feedback delivery also impacts the recipient's perceptions of and reactions to feedback.

FEEDBACK DELIVERY

The way in which feedback is delivered plays an important part in the feedback process. The feedback recipient's perceptions of and reactions to feedback are influenced not only by the actual feedback message and feedback source but also by how that feedback source provides the feedback—the medium, timing, frequency, and setting in which feedback is delivered.

The Medium

Feedback sources have many options for the medium, also referred to as the mechanism (e.g., as in Balcazar, Hopkins, & Suarez, 1985–1986), they use to deliver feedback. Several options for delivering feedback were identified in a review of a decade's worth of feedback research: graphs or figures (used to display performance data), verbal, written, mechanical (videotape), and combinations of all of them (Alvero, Bucklin, & Austin, 2001). The current research indicated that written feedback was the most commonly used medium. Alvero et al. (2001) found that a combination of media may be most effective for driving behavior change and that participants were most likely to follow through or take action on feedback when it was presented in the form of a graph or figure and paired with written or verbal feedback.

Written and verbal feedback can be reduced further to more specific modes of delivery. For example, written feedback could be a formal written performance appraisal document, an e-mail, comments in a Word document, comments from a social media site, or an instant message (IM) or text message. Moreover, verbal feedback can occur over the phone, in person, or even face-to-face via internet media like Skype, videoconference, or FaceTime on an iPad or iPhone. Advances in technology have dramatically impacted the frequency, immediacy, and availability of feedback exchanges—which can be both positive and negative. On the one hand, technology can enable "just-in-time" feedback that may allow the source to provide quick updates or allow the recipient the ability to course correct while working on something. When misused, though, technology can enable hasty interactions that are poorly thought through, and that may be destructive and favor efficiency over effectiveness. Try finding someone who has not quickly fired off a reactive text or e-mail and then immediately regretted it.

Waung and Highhouse (1997) found that feedback delivered via a direct medium (face-to-face) was more likely to be inflated than feedback delivered via an indirect medium (tape recorded). When negative feedback must be delivered face-to-face, the source may be uncomfortable or fearful of the recipient's reaction and, therefore, may water down his or her feedback and make it seem more positive than it actually is. This finding has important implications for consultants: They can work with clients to ensure that the true message and impact of challenging feedback do not get lost in poor delivery. It is important to be mindful of this effect and actively work with clients to help them overcome fear and avoidance of delivering difficult messages. A piece of advice that consultants can share with clients is to use a framework to structure feedback, such as the situation-behavior-impact model (SBI; the feedback describes the situation in which the behavior occurred, exactly what the behavior was, and why it matters—what the impact was; Weitzel, 2000); think ahead of time about exactly what they want to say; say it; and then stop talking. Often, people botch negative feedback messages by talking around the real issue or saying too much and leaving the recipient feeling unsure of exactly what the issue is or what they are supposed to do about it.

Au and Chan (2013) examined recipient preferences for feedback medium. They found that, even in this day of technology, sources and recipients still prefer face-to-face feedback over all other media, even when dealing with negative feedback. E-mail was the next most preferred medium, followed by telephone and then written communications other than e-mail. The same rank order (face-to-face, e-mail, telephone, written other than e-mail) was also found for the perceived usefulness of feedback. Au and Chan also found that people preferred lean media (i.e., e-mail, text, IM) when feedback was clear and unambiguous, and a richer medium (i.e., face-to-face and telephone in that particular study) for feedback that could potentially be misunderstood or that warranted more explanation.

In addition to the medium, the way that feedback is presented can also impact the way the recipient perceives and interprets it. For instance,

Stone et al. (1984) found that when both positive and negative feedback needed to be shared, presenting the positive feedback first followed by the negative feedback resulted in the recipient's perceiving both pieces of feedback as more accurate. Moreover, popular models, such as the SBI model or the STAR (situation, task, action, result) model can be useful for delivering feedback in a way that helps the recipient understand the exact situation in which the behavior occurred, exactly what the behavior was, and the impact of their behavior. For example, rather than just telling a colleague that he or she needs to have better presentation skills, a feedback provider could tell the colleague this:

> In last week's team meeting [situation], when you presented the results of the financial report [task], you read from your notes the entire time and didn't make eye contact with team members, and were very hard to hear because you mumbled throughout your entire presentation [action]. As a result, team members did not understand the key take-aways from the financial report, and you appeared to lack both competence and confidence in the results you were presenting [result].

This feedback, structured using the STAR model, allows the recipient to identify exactly his or her behavior, when it happened, and why it mattered. In addition, desired behavior can be tacked on to the end of SBI and STAR feedback. For example, this colleague could go on to say,

> Next time, look up from your notes, make eye contact with the team members, and speak louder and more clearly. That way everyone will know what great work you did on the financial report and leave the meeting understanding the key points of the financial report.

Including the desired behavior gives the recipient a jump start on making meaningful behavior change in response to the feedback.

Timing and Frequency

The timing and frequency of feedback delivery also shape recipients' perceptions and reactions. Ilgen et al. (1979) originally defined *timing* in feedback exchanges as the interval that elapses between the individual's action or behavior and his or her receipt of feedback about that action or behavior. In general, the longer the time interval, the smaller the effect of the feedback on performance (Hays, Kornell, & Bjork, 2013; van der Kleij, Eggen, Timmers, & Veldkamp, 2012). Hays et al. (2013) found that feedback provided immediately following failure on a task produced greater retention (e.g., memory of what caused the failure), whereas delayed feedback did not enhance retention. Similarly, van der Kleij et al. (2012) found that recipients paid more attention to immediate feedback than to delayed feedback. One could argue that, by the time delayed feedback is provided, it may be irrelevant or recipients have simply lost interest or moved on to something else.

Generally speaking, the longer the delay between the action or event and the feedback, the less likely it is that the individual will accurately recall the event. One reason why process feedback (see page 36) can be so valuable is because it is often provided just in time—it is delivered to individuals at the time they are working on the tasks for which feedback is provided. In such situations, the behavior is fresh in the recipient's mind, and he or she has immediate opportunities to take action on the feedback. Overall, feedback should be provided as soon as is reasonably possible after an event occurs, but in such a way that timeliness is balanced with effectiveness, such as choosing the right medium and the right situation in which to provide the feedback.

In addition to timing, the frequency with which feedback is provided can have positive effects on individual performance. Regular, informal feedback exchanges help people understand what they are doing well and where they have room to improve—often in manageable doses and in a time frame that allows them to apply feedback to their current performance (London, 2003). In many organizations, the bulk of feedback to staff is still delivered through infrequent, formal appraisal events, despite consistent findings on the importance of informal, frequent feedback (Corporate Leadership Council, 2012a). Kluger and DeNisi (1996) noted that frequent feedback messages result in more effective formal feedback interventions (e.g., annual performance appraisals). Similarly, frequent feedback reduces the likelihood that substantial gaps will exist long term between individual performance and organizational standards or expectations, thereby making formal performance appraisals feel more fair and accurate (Landy, Barnes, & Murphy, 1978; Taylor et al., 1984).

Feedback Delivery Setting

The setting in which feedback is delivered has implications for how the recipient will react to and act (or avoid acting) on that feedback. Feedback can be provided in either public (in front of others) or private (alone with the feedback provider) settings (Ashford & Northcraft, 1992; Levy, Albright, Cawley, & Williams, 1995). Receiving critical feedback in front of others can be embarrassing and can undermine an individual's attempts at maintaining a positive image. Ashford and Northcraft (1992) found that people are significantly less likely to seek feedback in public contexts, a finding that they attributed to the impression-management costs of seeking feedback and being vulnerable in front of peers or other important stakeholders. Levy et al. (1995) found similar results: In their research, individuals were also significantly less likely to seek feedback in a public versus a private setting.

However, research has also shown that, in some situations, using public feedback can have a positive impact. Ludwig, Biggs, Wagner, and Geller (2001) found that pizza delivery drivers had a 22% increase in safe driving behaviors over the course of several weeks, during which time feedback was publicly posted in the workplace about each driver's safety behaviors. Publicly posting feedback about every employee's behavior increased accountability and resulted in increased safety behavior. This public posting strategy can be effective for other types of behavior and performance. For example, Stephens and Ludwig (2005) found that glove-wearing rates increased from 61% to 93% when nurses were reminded to wear gloves when disposing of waste; the results of doing so were posted publicly. However, this approach should be used cautiously when targeting a specific individual's performance in contrast to feedback that pertains to an entire team or unit.

Feedback delivery is multifaceted. It includes attributes and behaviors of the feedback source (the who of feedback delivery), and the medium, timing, frequency, and setting in which the feedback is delivered (the how). Feedback providers need to be aware of the important role they play in the feedback process. In practice, consultants can help managers and other feedback providers understand the value in the feedback process of relationship building, cultivating trust, and showing support for their employees or other feedback recipients. Ultimately, any feedback exchange is an interpersonal event (London, 2003)—one that happens in the context of past experiences, existing relationships, and ongoing collaborations. In addition, clients or business partners will benefit from learning best practices for choosing when, where, and how to deliver feedback, such as selecting the right medium; providing feedback in the most timely manner possible; waiting until feedback can be delivered in private (as needed); and providing frequent, informal, just-in-time feedback. The next case study illustrates how feedback delivery variables can make or break the effectiveness of a new HR process.

PUTTING IT INTO PRACTICE

Introduced in the Introduction to this book, Ted works for a large global consulting firm and has extensive expertise and experience with organizational change, among other things. He recently was made part of a team that has been helping a client redesign its performance management system. Ted was brought on to help develop a strategy and process for getting HR business partners and managers on board with the new approach to performance management. Given his experience with change management, he brings a great deal of expertise to the team.

Ted's team members brief him on the new performance management process: The client has traditionally relied solely on an annual, stand-alone, formal performance appraisal in which employees are given a numerical rating on their performance and hear little else until the following year. Ted helps his organization move to an ongoing, less formal performance management approach, which emphasizes frequent feedback, a focus on employee growth and development, higher tolerance for risks and learn-ing by doing, and generally more manager–employee interactions, with the intention of building stronger manager–employee relationships.

In addition to helping plan and shape communications about the new performance management process and helping HR business partners and line managers understand their role in the process, Ted finds that, for the new performance management approach to succeed, these individuals need a lot of help learning how to give feedback. Initially, managers push back on the process and complain that it is too much work. To learn more and help manage the change, Ted conducts interviews with supervisors and concludes that the root issues are that managers are uncomfortable with the expectation to give so much feedback—particularly negative feedback. In response, Ted decides to focus a significant portion of the communication and training on how to deliver feedback, because that skill set is at the core of the ongoing, informal performance management process. He wants to take an evidence-based approach to the guidance he provides, so he turns to the research and best practices on how to deliver feedback most effectively.

Ted works with the team to develop a strategic curriculum that will be used to create written guides, just-in-time online learning modules, and in-person training sessions that will quickly increase the skill level of the HR business partners and line managers who will be responsible for bringing the new process to life. Ted and the team break the content into four major topics (see Figure 4.1): (1) the role of the feedback provider (touching on source credibility—including expertise and trustworthiness), (2) relationship building, (3) the various ways to deliver feedback (the medium—how to frame feedback, such as via the SBI model), and (4) when to give feedback (i.e., timing, frequency, setting—public vs. private).

The written guides and online training modules are designed to be available to HR business partners and line managers when they have quick questions or need guidance before talking to an employee about performance. The content appearing in the guides and online also is included in the in-person training session, which all HR business partners and line managers are expected to attend. In the training, participants learn

	Written Guides	Online Modules	In-Person Training
Your role as feedback provider	GUIDE 1: The 'who'	Module 1	All part of the half-day session
Relationship building		Module 2	
Ways to deliver feedback	GUIDE 2: The 'how'	Module 3	
When to give feedback		Module 4	

Figure 4.1

Ted's plan for delivering learning content that will quickly build the skills of HR business partners and line managers.

about the importance of their role in the process: that they need to establish credibility with their teams by demonstrating (and, in some cases, developing) expertise and showing themselves to be trustworthy. They learn that becoming familiar with their employees' performance, investing time in getting to know them, and knowing what they are working on will build their credibility and their relationships with their employees. They learn ways to build trust with their employees, such as keeping an employee's best intentions in mind when providing feedback, being honest and straightforward, and following through on things they say they will do. They are encouraged to actively demonstrate support for their employees by allowing them to take risks and make mistakes, so long as they learn from them, and helping them think through ways to target their development needs or change course when things are not going as well as they could be. One significant shift for these participants is the emphasis on building relationships and investing time with employees. The organization had tended to promote a more task-oriented culture, so this new process now requires HR business partners and managers to change the way they approach their day-to-day work.

Members of the organization's talent management team are responsible for owning the new process and the guides and training that Ted has helped design. However, to ensure that they are fully prepared, Ted co-leads the first several in-person training sessions with the talent management team. He built practice time into the training course so that participants would have the chance to practice their new feedback skills with each another.

Rolling out a new performance management process can be a daunting task. Ted and the talent management encountered challenges and pushback, particularly from line leaders, and are realistic in their expectations that it may take a few years for the process to become fully embedded and successful within the organization. However, they believe that the new process will lead to important changes in the ways that managers and their staff interact, and ultimately in individual performance and staff contributions.

CONCLUSION

The way that feedback is delivered can reinforce or negate the content of the actual feedback message. The source of the feedback plays a critical role in the feedback process and in the recipient's interpretation and reaction to that feedback. It is important to recognize the impact the source has on the feedback process. In many cases, challenges in feedback exchanges may uncover much bigger issues, such as ineffective work relationships, poor communication skills, and a failure to cultivate trust. The old adage that perception is reality is relevant to feedback exchanges; an important feedback message can be quickly diluted, downplayed, or rendered ineffective by the way in which it is delivered.

So far, we have discussed the content and delivery of the message. Another vital part of the feedback process concerns the recipient. Chapter 5 focuses on the individual differences of the recipient that play a role in the feedback process. After all, any feedback exchange is—at its core—simply an interpersonal interaction between the source and the recipient.

5

Perception Is Reality: The Role of Individual Differences in the Feedback Process

We have noted that the actual feedback message is only one component of the feedback exchange. The relationship and interpersonal interactions between the feedback provider and the feedback recipient also influence how that feedback is perceived and what outcomes or behaviors will result. As we discussed in Chapter 3, attributes of the feedback provider have a substantial impact on the feedback exchange. People are not merely passive recipients of feedback, but active participants in the process (Ashford & Cummings, 1983; Linderbaum & Levy, 2010). Now we turn our attention to the other half of that relationship: the qualities of the feedback recipient that affect how he or she is likely to perceive, interpret, and respond to feedback. So far, we have focused mainly on giving feedback, but how feedback is ultimately received is just as critical for an effective feedback process.

http://dx.doi.org/10.1037/14619-006
Using Feedback in Organizational Consulting, by J. B. Gregory and P. E. Levy

Each of the classic models presented in this book addresses the importance of considering individual differences of the feedback recipient to understand the feedback process (Ilgen, Fisher, & Taylor, 1979; Kluger & DeNisi, 1996; London & Smither, 2002; Taylor, Fisher, & Ilgen, 1984). Referring again to our simple model (see Figure 1.5), the feedback recipient is one of the critical components of the overall feedback process. Researchers have been investigating the role of individual differences and experiences for more than 6 decades. For example, Waterhouse and Child (1953) found that the effect of negative feedback on subsequent performance depends on how easily someone is frustrated. People bring their past experiences, expectations, and particular qualities with them into every feedback exchange. Ultimately, it is their perception of the feedback message and the way in which it is delivered that really matters—not just the actual content of the message or the source's intentions. Ilgen et al. (1979) suggested that the individual's frame of reference is "the major variable" (p. 356) that impacts perception of the feedback exchange. Individual differences, such as locus of control, self-esteem, personality, and motivation, affect perceptions of and reactions to feedback.

LOCUS OF CONTROL

Locus of control is the extent to which people think that they have personal control over the outcomes in their life (i.e., internal locus of control) or if those outcomes are primarily the result of outside forces, chance, or other factors outside of their control (i.e., external locus of control; Rotter, 1966). The effect of locus of control on perceptions of, and reactions to, feedback often depends on the specifics of the situation. For example, Baron, Cowan, and Ganz (1974) found that individuals with an internal locus of control had higher subsequent performance when they sought feedback on their own, but that individuals with an external locus of control had higher subsequent performance after receiving praise from another person. Baron and Ganz (1972) also found that individuals exhibited higher performance when feedback complemented their locus of control. Individuals with an internal locus of control have higher subsequent performance when they receive feedback that reinforces that internal control, whereas individuals with an external locus of control have higher performance when feedback touches on extrinsic factors of performance. People who have an external locus of control (also referred to as "externals") react more negatively to failure feedback than do internals and, as a result, make more excuses for their performance (Basgall & Snyder, 1988). Individuals with an external locus of control may feel as though failure "happened" to them, thereby underestimating their role in the failure. They may feel frustrated by receiving negative feedback when they feel like the failure was not their fault.

Having a sense of personal control over outcomes factors into how people respond to feedback—particularly negative feedback. Having an external locus of control results in more negative reactions to failure feedback (Basgall & Snyder, 1988; Lam & Schaubroeck, 2000). When people believe that factors outside of their control are responsible for their actions or important outcomes, negative feedback directed at their behavior is likely to incite feelings of defensiveness and a tendency to reject feedback. On the other hand, for individuals with an internal locus of control, having a sense of personal control contributes to a feeling of competence, which is also an important element of intrinsic motivation (i.e., being motivated by internal forces, as opposed to external rewards; Deci, 1975; White, 1959). Ilgen et al. (1979) noted that the motivational value of feedback (e.g., the extent to which it motivates behavior or effort) is impacted by this sense of competence and personal control. When people feel competent and believe they have control over a situation, feedback is more likely to motivate them to action, presumably because they believe they are capable of taking that action. In addition, people are less likely to give up following failure feedback if they are able to attribute that failure to lack of effort, rather than to lack of ability (Dweck, 1975). Effort is considered an unstable factor—something that can be changed and is not necessarily consistent across situations. In contrast, attributing outcomes or results to ability, which is more stable and perceived to be less controllable than effort, may increase the negativity of the reaction to feedback. Attributing failure to unstable factors, such as level of effort, allows individuals to believe they exert personal control over outcomes simply by increasing that level of effort. However, when individuals believe that their failures resulted from lack of ability, they are more inclined to believe that they are not able to improve, because their ability is fixed (i.e., stable). The way that individuals explain or attribute their performance (e.g., to internal vs. external causes, to stable vs. unstable factors) impacts how they respond to negative feedback.

SELF-ESTEEM AND SELF-EFFICACY

Another individual difference variable that is important in the feedback process is *self-esteem*, a person's overall sense of self-worth (Coopersmith, 1967). Self-esteem particularly impacts how people respond to negative feedback. Research has demonstrated that after receiving negative feedback, individuals with high self-esteem exerted more effort on subsequent tasks, whereas individuals with low self-esteem had an even worse performance on subsequent tasks (Fedor, Davis, Maslyn, & Mathieson, 2001; Shrauger & Rosenberg, 1970). After receiving positive feedback on their performance, individuals with high self-esteem also improved their performance more than individuals with low self-esteem. Having confidence in one's abilities essentially buffers against the emotional blow that often comes with negative feedback. Kluger and DeNisi (1996) suggested that negative feedback is more likely to direct attention inward for individuals with low self-esteem, thereby further activating their self-doubt and inward focus rather than a focus on improving the task at hand. Individuals with low self-confidence may be more likely to engage in ego-protecting behavior (e.g., avoiding negative feedback) rather than focusing on the task at hand, whereas individuals with high self-confidence will likely be more open to task-related feedback (London, 2003) for its informational value and utility for learning and developing.

Similarly, self-efficacy impacts how individuals respond to and use feedback. *Self-efficacy* differs from self-esteem in that it pertains to an individual's belief that he or she has the skills and capability necessary to complete a particular task (Bandura, 1986). Feedback and self-efficacy have a somewhat reciprocal relationship. On the one hand, feedback can help build self-efficacy by reinforcing behavior and helping individuals gain confidence in their behavior. Vancouver and colleagues (Vancouver & Kendall, 2006; Vancouver, More, & Yoder, 2008; Vancouver, Thompson, Tischner, & Putka, 2002) have consistently found that positive feedback contributes to higher self-efficacy, which in turn can lead to setting higher and more challenging goals and, as a result, higher levels of performance.[1] On the other hand, people are more motivated to use feedback for development when they have high self-efficacy (Colquitt, LePine, & Noe, 2000; London, 2003). Individuals with high self-efficacy are more likely to accept the feedback they receive and also are more likely to proactively seek feedback (Brown, Ganesan, & Challagalla, 2001). This effect is consistent for the delivery of upward feedback, such as when a supervisor receives feedback from subordinates or direct reports. Upward feedback results in greater subsequent performance when the recipient has high self-efficacy (Heslin, Latham, & VandeWalle, 2005). When individuals believe that they possess the capability to respond to and act on feedback, they will be more open to and accepting of that feedback. Like those with low self-esteem, individuals with low self-efficacy may be more prone to ego-protecting mechanisms (London, 2003), such as avoiding or dismissing negative feedback or feedback that is inconsistent with their self-perception. A high level of self-efficacy, or belief in one's capabilities, should make people more open to, accepting of, and inclined to use feedback. Reinforcing feedback, in turn, can help build self-efficacy with time.

For consulting psychologists, it is important to be aware of the important role that self-esteem and self-efficacy play in the feedback process for individuals. These variables affect the way in which individual clients react to and act on feedback, and thus play a critical role in important outcomes, such as development or performance improvement. Depending on the particular client or situation, consulting psychologists may want to incorporate formal assessments of self-esteem or global self-efficacy into their practice to better understand the client's perspective. For clients who

---

[1]However, performance has also been shown to decline once a certain level of self-efficacy has been achieved, because individuals may feel a reduced need to devote time, effort, and preparation to tasks in which they assume they will be successful (Vancouver et al., 2008).

struggle with self-esteem or self-efficacy, personal development goals could focus on developing these important beliefs, both of which are best developed by taking on stretch goals and demonstrating competence to oneself.

PERSONALITY

Traditional personality variables also play a role in how individuals perceive and react to feedback. The overwhelming majority of this research has focused on the Big Five model of personality, which consists of five dimensions: (1) Agreeableness, (2) Conscientiousness, (3) Extraversion, (4) Neuroticism, and (5) Openness to Experience (McCrae & Costa, 1999). Although findings have been somewhat inconsistent (Walker et al., 2010), both conscientiousness and neuroticism have been shown to have an effect on feedback-related behavior. People who are high on conscientiousness, for example, tend to be more motivated to use feedback for development purposes (Colquitt et al., 2000) and also have higher performance after receiving feedback from peers (Dominick, Reilly, & Byrne, 2004). Similarly, Smither, London, and Richmond (2005) found that one particular aspect of conscientiousness—responsibility—predicted a sense of obligation to use feedback and increased feedback-seeking behavior and development, even 6 months after receiving multisource feedback. In his research into the feedback-seeking personality, Krasman (2010) found that conscientiousness, neuroticism, and extraversion predicted increased feedback-seeking behavior (e.g., individuals actively seeking feedback from supervisors).

Neuroticism, however, has also been associated with worsened performance following negative feedback (Robinson, Moeller, & Fetterman, 2010). Overall, the higher people's level of neuroticism (also referred to as emotional stability; high levels of neuroticism would be described as low emotional stability, and vice versa), the worse their performance after receiving negative feedback. On the other hand, people with low levels of neuroticism (i.e., high emotional stability) tend to be more motivated to use the feedback that they receive (Colquitt et al., 2000; Smither et al., 2005). Because neuroticism and anxiety are closely connected, it is possible that the emotional stress of receiving negative feedback creates a great deal of anxiety for individuals with high levels of neuroticism. This anxiety can interfere with their ability to mindfully process feedback and to perform (let alone make improvements in performance). People with high levels of social anxiety tend to perceive feedback as more negative than do individuals with low levels of social anxiety (Smith & Sarason, 1975). For example, if a person gives Chris and Jared the exact same feedback message, Chris—who has a high level of social anxiety—will rate that feedback message as more negative than will Jared, who has a low level of social anxiety. Trait levels of anxiety not only have effects on how individuals respond to and use feedback but also color their perception and interpretation of that feedback.

In addition to traits, evidence suggests that an individual's states can play a role in his or her perceptions of feedback (Shute, 2008; Strijbos, Narciss, & Dünnebier, 2010). When feedback is consistent with someone's mood (e.g., negative feedback is provided to someone in a negative mood), that person is more likely to perceive the feedback as accurate than when it is inconsistent with their mood (e.g., negative feedback provided to someone in a positive mood; Hammer & Stone-Romero, 1996). People in a positive mood state are likely to perceive positive feedback they receive as being more accurate then negative feedback. Similarly, people in a negative mood are more inclined to perceive negative feedback as accurate. People also tend to process negative feedback more deeply when they are already experiencing a negative mood (Ingram, 1984). Negative emotions have been shown to narrow thinking and bring one's focus to a lower level of detail (Fredrickson & Branigan, 2005), which has interesting implications for practice. Clients or employees who are in a very positive mood might be more inclined to perceive negative feedback as inaccurate, and vice versa. Before delivering negative feedback, for example, managers may need to make an effort to set the tone for the conversation to help individuals adjust their emotional states to match the situation. Jumping right in to negative feedback with jovial employees may impact their perception of the feedback and make them less likely to accept and take action on that feedback. Managers or consultants may need to ease into the conversation by providing sufficient context and—as perverse as it sounds—trying to influence and shape the employee or client's mood to be slightly less positive. For example, starting the conversation with a discussion—using a frank and negative tone—of the situation or context will signal to the employee or client that the individual feedback to follow will not be positive. This approach will allow the employee or client's mood to shift accordingly, thus preparing the individual for the negative feedback.

MOTIVATION

People have unique preferences for and perspectives on what motivates them. One individual difference variable that can have a significant impact on motivation is regulatory focus. *Promotion-focused* people tend to be motivated to achieve successes and ideals, whereas *prevention-focused* people are more motivated to avoid negative outcomes (Higgins, 2000). Promotion-focused individuals are more sensitive and attuned to positive stimuli, whereas the same is true of prevention-focused individuals regarding negative stimuli. In addition, *regulatory fit*—the extent to which the feedback matches an individual's regulatory focus—further affects motivation and performance. *Regulatory focus* influences how people frame their goals and whether they tend to be more motivated by achieving success or avoiding failure. Idson and Higgins (2000) found that individuals had higher subsequent performance after receiving feedback that was consistent with their regulatory focus (e.g., success feedback for promotion-oriented people, failure feedback for prevention-oriented people) compared with those who received feedback that was inconsistent with their regulatory focus orientation. Clear evidence suggests that promotion-focused people tend to be more motivated by positive feedback, whereas prevention-focused people are more motivated by negative feedback (Förster, Grant, Idson, & Higgins, 2001; Van-Dijk & Kluger, 2004). When feedback is written or presented in such a way to match an individual's regulatory focus, that feedback is more readily accepted and more likely to result in higher levels of motivation (Jarzebowski, Palermo, & van de Berg, 2012); in effect, feedback matching one's regulatory focus is likely to be more effective. Regulatory focus can be easily assessed through self-report measures, something that consulting psychologists may want to consider adding to their practice.

A related concept shown to impact individual performance following feedback is goal orientation. *Goal orientation* corresponds to an individual's tendency to be more motivated by either learning (mastery) or performance (Dweck, 1986; Elliott & Dweck, 1988). People who have a dispositional *learning goal orientation* tend to focus more on learning, attaining mastery at tasks, and acquiring new skills, whereas *performance-oriented* people are more motivated to demonstrate their competence or abilities to others. VandeWalle (2003) suggested that individuals who tend toward a learning goal orientation would be more interested in process (as opposed to outcome) feedback and emphasized the value and utility of actively seeking feedback. Performance-oriented individuals, however, would be more likely to avoid getting feedback after the occurrence of a negative event (in which they did not effectively demonstrate their competence), more likely to avoid getting feedback from expert sources, and more likely to focus on the costs of seeking feedback (e.g., damage to one's image by asking for feedback). Interestingly, people with a learning goal orientation may be more motivated after receiving negative feedback, rather than positive feedback, because of its informational value. For example, Cianci, Schaubroeck, and McGill (2010) found that individuals working toward learning-framed goals they had set had higher levels of subsequent performance after receiving negative feedback. Negative feedback can be used to quickly learn and enhance performance, whereas positive feedback simply reinforces what individuals are already doing and does not motivate them to increase effort or performance. In most cases, accurate negative feedback provides more diagnostic value—it helps people better understand their strengths and weaknesses with special emphasis on identifying where performance needs to improve. Diagnostic process feedback is often most sought after by learning goal-oriented individuals, because they want whatever information they can get that will identify how they can get better, and negative process feedback has those diagnostic elements.

FEEDBACK ORIENTATION

One of the most relevant individual difference variables when it comes to feedback is an individual's feedback orientation (Linderbaum & Levy, 2010; London & Smither, 2002). This construct was first introduced just more than a decade ago in London and Smither's (2002) seminal paper about the feedback process. An individual's *feedback orientation* refers to the extent to which he or she likes, values, and feels accountable to use feedback. Feedback orientation affects how receptive people are to feedback and the extent to which they are open to receiving guidance and coaching. Individuals with a favorable feedback orientation are more likely to have a positive attitude toward feedback, actively seek it out, process the feedback deeply and mindfully, be aware of how others perceive them, find value in feedback, and feel a sense of accountability to do something with the feedback they receive (London & Smither, 2002). London and Smither noted that feedback orientation is related to several other variables described in this chapter—self-confidence, self-esteem, and learning or mastery orientation—and also that it can be developed or improved over time.

Linderbaum and Levy (2010) built on the work of London and Smither (2002) to develop a measure of feedback orientation: the Feedback Orientation Scale (FOS). Linderbaum and Levy identified four dimensions of feedback orientation: (1) utility (finding value in using feedback), (2) accountability (feeling accountable to do something with feedback), (3) self-awareness (being aware of how others perceive you), and (4) feedback self-efficacy (believing that you have the capability to do something with the feedback). The FOS is a self-report measure that individuals can use to assess their feedback orientation. Individuals can grow in their appreciation for, and level of comfort with, feedback. An individual's feedback orientation impacts how open he or she is to coaching (e.g., from a manager or executive coach). However, effective coaching can help develop feedback orientation, making clients more open to and accepting of feedback, and more likely to see the value and utility of feedback. Gregory and Levy (2012) found that a coachee's feedback orientation predicted the quality of the coaching relationship, which is considered a prerequisite to effective coaching. When clients or employees have favorable feedback orientations, they are likely more open to coaching and thus share a higher quality relationship with a coach or coaching manager, which leads to more effective coaching.

Feedback orientation also shares a reciprocal relationship with an important contextual variable: feedback environment (London & Smither, 2002; Steelman, Levy, & Snell, 2004), which is discussed extensively in Chapter 6. Feedback environments[2] are shaped by the day-to-day feedback-related behavior in an organization or work group. In a favorable feedback environment, employees regularly receive constructive feedback, seek feedback from peers and superiors, and use feedback to continuously improve their performance. London and Smither (2002) suggested that a reciprocal relationship also exists between a feedback environment and individuals' feedback orientations. Working in a favorable feedback environment can lead to the growth and development of individual employees' feedback orientations (a top-down effect). Similarly, a group of employees with favorable feedback orientations who work together and consistently give, seek, and use feedback will create a favorable feedback environment for that work group or organization (a bottom-up effect). Research has consistently demonstrated a strong relationship between these two variables (Dahling, Chau, & O'Malley, 2012; Gregory, 2010; Linderbaum & Levy, 2010). Leaders and managers also have a great deal of influence on shaping the feedback environment for a work group or organization by setting the tone and establishing expectations for how feedback will be used in the workplace. Managers who provide frequent and informal feedback to their employees, who encourage those employees to actively seek feedback from others, and who hold employees accountable to learn from and act on feedback create a favorable feedback environment through these actions. In doing so, they are also helping to grow and strengthen the feedback orientations of each individual employee.

An array of individual difference variables impact the feedback process, including the ways in which individuals perceive, interpret, react to,

---

[2]*Feedback environment* is synonymous with *feedback culture*, the term used in London and Smither (2002).

and act (or fail to act) on feedback they receive. Understanding the important role of individual differences will help consultants be more effective in working with organizations and individuals in situations involving feedback. Consider clients' individual differences when delivering feedback to them, and educate leaders and managers within client organizations to become more aware of the important role of individual differences in feedback exchanges.

PUTTING IT INTO PRACTICE

In the Introduction to this book, we introduced Sylvia, a consulting psychologist who works for a small firm that specializes in executive assessment. She spends a great deal of time consulting with client organizations that want assessments of current leaders or candidates for leadership positions so they can identify the best candidates for hire or succession and develop their current or future leaders. Over the years, Sylvia has learned through experience how important it is to consider individual differences when providing assessment feedback to clients. She has learned to invest time in getting to know her clients before delivering feedback so that she may tailor her approach to their attitudes, expectations, and tendencies toward feedback. Failing to do so increases the likelihood that clients will get defensive, be dismissive, and be less inclined to use feedback for personal development and improved performance.

A private equity firm has hired Sylvia to provide developmental assessments to the top seven leaders of a financial services organization recently acquired by the firm. The private equity firm believes these leaders have the capability to grow the business, but not without significant investment in the leaders' development and capacity to better motivate and inspire their small workforce. Each leader will work with an executive coach for 6 to 12 months, but only after going through an intensive assessment process with Sylvia's firm, which partners with the executive coaches to ensure continuity.

Each leader completes a battery of online assessments, which includes measures of personality, cognitive ability, learning agility, motivation, and potential derailers. After completing the assessment battery, each leader has a 1-hour interview with one of Sylvia's colleagues, who inquires about past job experiences, relationships at work, concerns about current and future challenges, and self-perceptions. In addition, Sylvia's firm conducts multisource feedback (i.e., 360° feedback) interviews for each leader: talking with peers, direct reports, and the company president to whom the leaders report. Another colleague at Sylvia's firm synthesizes the data from the assessment battery, one-on-one interview, and multisource interviews into a detailed report. Sylvia sets up time with each of the seven leaders to provide feedback and help them get the greatest possible value from their assessment report.

As Sylvia prepares for her meeting with Elizabeth, the organization's director of risk and compliance, she spends time reviewing the assessment results to get a feel for Elizabeth's personality and motivations. The assessment battery did not measure all of the individual difference variables that have been examined in feedback research, but it did provide important insights on variables, such as Elizabeth's personality (high conscientious, high neuroticism), motivational orientations (learning/mastery oriented, moderately prevention oriented), and trait affect (moderately high levels of social anxiety). Sylvia also concludes from the assessment and other data that Elizabeth has a strong internal locus of control. Sylvia knows from experience that she can get a sense for an individual's feedback orientation, self-esteem, and self-efficacy by asking relevant questions at the beginning of a session.

Sylvia joins Elizabeth in her office for a 2-hour session in which they review the assessment report and discuss development goals and priorities on which Elizabeth will focus over the next several months as she works with her executive coach. Sylvia has planned to dedicate the first 30 minutes of their meeting to getting acquainted and asking questions that will help Sylvia to understand how Elizabeth generally handles feedback. Sylvia jots down notes on Elizabeth as they talk to stay mindful of how Elizabeth might react to and interpret feedback that Sylvia provides (see Figure 5.1).

To diagnose Elizabeth's feedback orientation, Sylvia asks questions inspired by Linderbaum and Levy's (2010) FOS, such as, "How do you typically act on feedback that you receive?" (the accountability dimension

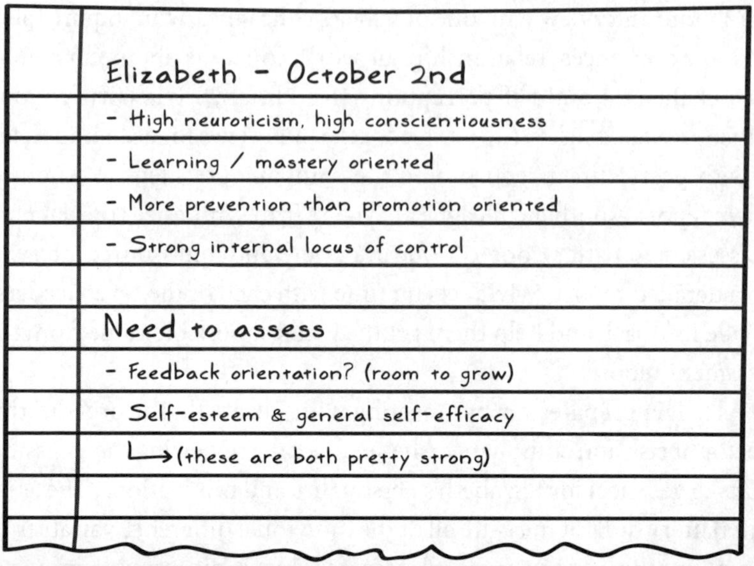

Figure 5.1

Sylvia's coaching notes for working with Elizabeth.

of feedback orientation) and "What insights have you gained about the way others perceive you, based on feedback that you have received?" (the social awareness dimension of feedback orientation). Sylvia also inquires about Elizabeth's sense of self-worth (i.e., self-esteem) and general self-efficacy by asking about her work and the challenges she encounters, and how confident and prepared she feels about confronting those challenges. Overall, Sylvia concludes that Elizabeth has high self-esteem and high general self-efficacy, but has some room to further develop and improve her feedback orientation. Based on results of the 360° report, Elizabeth tends to come across as aloof and sometimes discounts the input of others, which might prevent her from getting the most out of feedback provided by her peers or colleagues.

After taking time to get acquainted, Sylvia and Elizabeth begin reviewing the assessment results. Elizabeth is interested in gaining new insights and self-awareness from the assessment process, but Sylvia suspects that Elizabeth might be more open than usual because her success with the company has depended largely on her ability to show rapid development and improvement in better inspiring and connecting with her staff. Sylvia is mindful of Elizabeth's tendencies to be somewhat neurotic and prevention focused (e.g., in setting goals, she tends to try to avoid failure rather than strive for successes), but Sylvia also recognizes that Elizabeth's mastery orientation and high self-efficacy could serve as a buffer against any strong emotional reactions to negative feedback. Sylvia is transparent with Elizabeth about the role of personality and individual differences in accepting and using feedback—both of which could impact her interactions with colleagues, personal development, and job performance. Sylvia spends time discussing Elizabeth's high levels of neuroticism and conscientiousness, and the meaning of these two personality dimensions. She also asks Elizabeth to think of examples of how these facets of her personality have impacted her work and interactions. Elizabeth notes that she has a tendency to "fixate" on challenges or problems—even when they are minor—and can see how these aspects of her personality might contribute to this behavior. Sylvia then discusses feedback from Elizabeth's one-on-one interview and the multisource interviews, and notes how the theme of focusing on small details seems to frustrate her direct reports and also distracts Elizabeth from more important matters.

Elizabeth is initially defensive in response to negative feedback from her multisource interviews. Sylvia reminds her that it is normal for people to have a strong emotional reaction to negative feedback, but if she can get past that emotional reaction and think of examples of the behavior, she will be able to identify clear opportunities for growth and development. Because Elizabeth has an internal locus of control and high self-efficacy, Sylvia feels confident that, once Elizabeth has identified a development goal, she will be successful in pursuing and achieving it. During the conversation, Sylvia invests time in educating Elizabeth on the value of feedback, with the intention of planting the seeds for growing and developing her feedback orientation over the course of her executive coaching engagement.

At the conclusion of their time together, Elizabeth is open to getting started on her personal development plans. On the basis of the feedback she has received from the executive assessment process, she identifies areas to focus her personal development. She plans to think more about exactly where she wants to focus and why, and, in her first session with her executive coach, Helen, with whom Sylvia frequently partners, talks in detail about cementing those plans. Sylvia assures Elizabeth that their conversation is confidential, but asks whether she could talk about their time together with Helen, who will receive a copy of the assessment report. Elizabeth is comfortable with this request and sees the value of bringing Helen up to speed on the discussion.

Before Helen's first coaching session with Elizabeth, Sylvia shares her observations with Helen. Sylvia believes that Elizabeth will set meaningful development goals and actively pursue them, but that Helen might want to intentionally focus on helping Elizabeth develop her feedback orientation. Not only will a more favorable feedback orientation help Elizabeth's own performance and relationships, but, given her span of responsibility, it will also help to cultivate a more positive feedback environment in her functional area of the business. Sylvia and Helen agree that better interactions with her employees and a more positive feedback environment in her part of the business will help Elizabeth achieve the results that their investors want to see: better leadership and more inspired employees, which ultimately will help to drive improved business performance. Certainly these changes will not occur overnight, but, with clear feedback and progress on her development plan, Elizabeth will achieve incremental progress.

CONCLUSION

Sylvia combined strong science with best practice in drawing on her knowledge of the role that individual differences play in the feedback process. In an ideal world, she would have been able to formally assess all of the individual differences discussed in this chapter. However, given practical constraints, Sylvia was resourceful in her use of executive assessment data and careful conversation with Elizabeth to understand how she might react to and use feedback based on her personality, past experiences, motivational approach, and other unique characteristics. The value of feedback largely depends on the way in which the recipient perceives and interprets that feedback. Two individuals may receive the exact same feedback message but, based on their attitudes, personality, experiences, and expectations, interpret it in different ways. Coaches and consultants should be mindful of the lens through which their clients are interpreting feedback that they or others provide. They should consider and work with each individual's unique differences when providing or discussing feedback. By tailoring their approach, consulting psychologists can shape the feedback experience for each client. They should seek first to understand each client as an individual, then focus on presenting feedback and asking questions that will allow clients to get the most value possible out of the feedback experience.

Thus far, we have discussed elements of the actual feedback message, the role of the feedback source and how he or she delivers feedback, and the importance of the recipient's individual differences. Feedback is never delivered in a vacuum; the situation in which it is provided also plays a role in the overall feedback process. We next turn our attention to the role of context in the feedback process.

6

Context Matters

No feedback exchange takes place in a vacuum. In addition to existing relationships, past experiences, and individual differences, the social context or environment in which exchange occurs also plays a role in the feedback process. The role of the situation or environment in human behavior is a fundamental tenet of psychology (Myers, 2010). The context of a situation influences the ways in which people perceive events, things, and other people, and also how we think and act. Behavior within organizations—including feedback-related behavior—is no exception. Early feedback research, such as several of the foundational articles reviewed in Chapter 1 (Ilgen, Fisher, & Taylor, 1979; Kluger & DeNisi, 1996; Taylor, Fisher, & Ilgen, 1984), did not emphasize the role of the organizational context in their models of the feedback process. Ilgen et al. (1979) discussed the importance of the environment as one potential source of feedback, but they did not talk more broadly about the effect of the environment on the

http://dx.doi.org/10.1037/14619-007
Using Feedback in Organizational Consulting, by J. B. Gregory and P. E. Levy
Copyright © 2015 by the American Psychological Association. All rights reserved.

feedback process. Similarly, Kluger and DeNisi (1996) discussed the environment as a valuable source of information and also noted that learning environments that provide feedback and allow for trial and error can be a good alternative for more direct feedback interventions. However, they went no further in addressing the role of the environment in feedback interventions.

In the past 10 to 15 years, though, a strong body of research has begun to enhance an understanding of the role that context plays in the feedback process. That research has much to offer to the practice of consulting psychology by clarifying the situations in which people are more or less likely to actively seek feedback and by demonstrating the positive effects of a favorable feedback environment on an array of important work outcomes. Referring to our simple model (see Figure 5.1), context is the fourth critical component of the feedback process. In this chapter, we discuss the role of context in individual feedback-seeking behavior, examine the role that organizational culture plays in the feedback process, and focus extensively on one particular component of organizational culture: an organization's feedback environment.

FEEDBACK SEEKING AND CONTEXT

Most people are motivated to manage the impressions they make on others. People will actively monitor their behavior so that others will view them in a positive light, and most people generally avoid engaging in behaviors that might lead others to question their abilities or competence, or make them come across as insecure (Ashford & Northcraft, 1992; Williams, Miller, Steelman, & Levy, 1999). In general, people are less likely to actively seek feedback in a public context than in a private setting. Ashford and Northcraft (1992) suggested that people weigh the costs and benefits of seeking feedback before actually doing so. Certainly, actively seeking feedback from others has a number of benefits, such as learning how to improve one's performance or reducing uncertainty. However, individuals may also feel deterred by the potential costs of seeking feedback, such as being perceived as incompetent, appearing to be insecure or uncertain, and experiencing the potential embarrassment of receiving negative feedback in front of others.

Interestingly, Ashford and Northcraft (1992) found that people who sought feedback were viewed in a positive light, thus indicating that their self-conscious concerns about impression management were unwarranted. The important takeaway from that research is that, regardless of what others actually think, people still seek less feedback in a public context because of perceived costs related to how they believe they might come across to others. People are more likely to report feeling nervous about seeking feedback in public, as opposed to private, and even more nervous when that public context includes an element of evaluation. Ashford and Northcraft also found that organizational norms for feedback seeking—that is, accepted and expected behavior for feedback seeking in the organization—also influenced how often individuals seek feedback. When organizational norms encouraged feedback seeking, individuals sought significantly more feedback than when organizational norms for feedback seeking were lower.

Replicating those results, Levy, Albright, Cawley, and Williams (1995) found that individuals were significantly less likely to actively seek feedback in a public setting. They also found that people who had intentions to seek feedback were more likely to reconsider those intentions and modify their behavior in a public setting. Even people who were interested in and intended to seek feedback would be less likely to do so in a public setting, such as in front of peers or coworkers. Levy et al. also found that feedback seeking in public contexts showed a decreasing trend over time. When given multiple opportunities to seek feedback, individuals in a public context will seek some feedback at first, but seek less and less with subsequent opportunities in that same public setting. The exact opposite was true for private contexts: Individuals in a private setting will seek more feedback over time in a given situation. As an example, an employee who is part of a 2-hour-long team meeting might seek some feedback at the start of the meeting but will seek less and less in front of peers as the meeting continues. On the other hand, if that same employee has a 2-hour meeting with his or her manager, he or she may seek even more feedback as the conversation progresses, because the employee perceives this setting as more private.

Expanding on those findings, Williams et al. (1999) also demonstrated that people seek less feedback in public settings. They found that supervisor support and positive peer reactions in response to feedback seeking in a public context led to increased feedback seeking. Even in a public context, if individuals believed that their managers and peers were supportive, they would continue to actively seek feedback from those sources. People were more inclined to actively seek feedback in a private setting, where they did not need to feel concerned with managing the impressions that they were conveying to others. However, in a public context, people could be encouraged to seek more feedback when they felt that their manager and peers were supportive, and when organizational norms encouraged feedback seeking. By being supportive in the way feedback was delivered and being timely in its delivery, researchers were able to create a context in which participants were much more likely to seek feedback in public than they were in conditions in which experimenters were neither timely nor supportive.

ORGANIZATIONAL CULTURE

Organizational norms shape and are shaped by the larger, overarching organizational culture, which generally includes the shared beliefs, values, and behavioral norms within an organization (Cooke & Rousseau, 1988). Organizational cultures set the tone for how employees collectively act and approach their work. The extent to which organizations espouse and cultivate a learning culture (i.e., learning organizations) or a culture for development will impact the ways in which managers and employees approach feedback. When organizations provide resources and opportunities for development, and hold employees accountable to continuously learn and develop, they cultivate a culture for development. Maurer, Mitchell, and Barbeite (2002) found that managers are significantly more likely to participate in and encourage development when the organization actively supports employee development. Organizational support for development is essential for continuous learning (London & Smither, 1999), and learning opportunities are more likely to transfer to job performance when the organizational culture supports learning and development (Tracey, Tannenbaum, & Kavanagh, 1995).

Learning organizations are those in which employees have opportunities for team learning and to build their personal mastery, and in which they share a long-term vision, engage in systems thinking, and share similar mental models (Senge, 1990). Although a variety of definitions have been offered for learning organizations (Garvin, 1993; Marsick & Watkins, 1999; Pedler, Burgoyne, & Boydell, 1991; Yang, Watkins, & Marsick, 2004), they can generally be described as organizations that have a collective capacity for learning, adaptation, and change. In a synthesis of the many conceptualizations and definitions of learning organizations, Yang et al. (2004) identified several common themes, including person-level, structural-level, and outcome components of learning organizations. The people components of learning organizations include creating continuous learning opportunities, promoting inquiry (i.e., feedback seeking) and dialogue among employees, encouraging collaboration and team learning, and empowering people toward a collective vision. The structural components, on the other hand, include connecting the organization to the broader environment, establishing systems to capture and share learning, and providing strategic leadership for learning. Yang et al. found that these elements of learning organizations drive important outcomes, such as gains in organizational knowledge and increased financial performance.

The Yang et al. (2004) model of learning organizations highlights the importance of feedback through the promoting-inquiry-and-dialogue facet of their model. This dimension pertains to an organization's ability to create an environment in which employees feel comfortable asking questions of one another and the organization, regularly give and seek feedback, and experiment with different behaviors. Organizations with a strong learning culture emphasize continuous experimentation and feedback (London, 2003). Inherent in continuous learning is the need for ongoing feedback to help individuals understand what they are doing right and where they have room to improve their performance. Cultures that enable frequent, informal feedback exchanges across the hierarchy and from peer to peer encourage learning, growth, and development, which contribute to higher performance levels and more effective organizations.

FEEDBACK ENVIRONMENT

Organizations in which employees consistently receive, seek, and use feedback can be described as having a favorable feedback environment (London & Smither, 2002). The concept of the feedback environment has been of increasing interest to researchers over the past decade (Ashford & Northcraft, 2003; London & Smither, 2002; Steelman, Levy, & Snell, 2004). Feedback environment can be considered an element of organizational culture. Whereas an organization's culture encompasses many aspects of employee thinking and behavior, the feedback environment pertains specifically to feedback-related behaviors. Occasional references were made to the existence of a feedback culture or environment in the 1970s and 1980s (Ashford & Cummings, 1983; Greller & Herold, 1975; Hanser & Muchinsky, 1978; Herold & Parsons, 1985), but that research lacked a clear definition of what the feedback environment was and how it impacted employee behavior and organizational outcomes. Those early conceptualizations of the feedback environment focused on the availability of feedback—Is it provided often? Is it easy to access? (Herold & Parsons, 1985)—and feedback sign (generally suggesting that an abundance of positive feedback contributed to a desirable feedback environment). Feedback environment was also broadly defined as the amount of information available in the surrounding environment that could be used to understand how well or poorly an individual's performance aligned with expectations (Hanser & Muchinsky, 1978).

Since then, a more specific and widely agreed on definition of feedback environment has taken shape. Drawing on London and Smither (2002) and Steelman et al. (2004), feedback environment includes the day-to-day feedback process that takes place within organizations, primarily between supervisors and subordinates but also between colleagues. In a favorable feedback environment, individuals continuously receive feedback (both formal and informal) from others, they actively seek feedback from others, and they are expected to learn from and use the feedback they receive. In unfavorable feedback environments, individuals rarely receive feedback—perhaps only during stand-alone, formal annual performance appraisals—do not actively seek feedback, are not encouraged to give or seek feedback, and are not held accountable for acting on feedback they receive.

London and Smither (2002) identified three types of organizational practices that contribute to a favorable feedback environment. The first is practices that enhance the quality of feedback. They noted that employees will be more receptive to and less likely to dismiss feedback that conveys clear standards and links performance to desired organizational outcomes. Higher quality feedback throughout the organization can be achieved by training managers on how best to provide feedback to their employees and holding them accountable to do so. Second, certain organizational practices can help emphasize the important role that feedback plays in the organizations. Organizations can set expectations that leaders and managers need to be role models for giving, seeking, accepting, and using feedback. Clear expectations for giving frequent informal feedback and being accountable for use of that feedback will contribute to a favorable feedback environment. Third, a feedback environment can be enhanced by organizational practices that provide support for using feedback. Organizations can provide resources and opportunities for getting the greatest value out of feedback (e.g., facilitators for reviewing formal assessment feedback, such as 360° data). Managers can be trained to help employees turn feedback into development goals and actions. Developing coaching skills and capabilities throughout the organization will also help to grow the organization's feedback environment.

As mentioned in Chapter 5, a reciprocal relationship exists between individual feedback orientations and the organizational feedback environment. Feedback orientation is an individual difference variable that describes the extent to which an individual is receptive to and interested in feedback. There are top-down and bottom-up elements to this reciprocal relationship. For instance, the feedback environment in which people work can—over time—help to develop their feedback orientation, such that individuals with a weak or negative feedback orientation will benefit from working in a favorable feedback environment (London & Smither, 2002). Based on this top-down perspective, individual employees will be buoyed by the favorable environment in which constructive feedback is provided often and employees are encouraged to give, seek, and use feedback. In addition, individuals with a positive feedback orientation will flourish in a favorable feedback environment. Their desire for feedback and inclination to use feedback for development and improved performance will be well matched to a work environment that enables free and constructive use of feedback.

From a bottom-up perspective, an unfavorable feedback environment can be made more favorable over time when managers and staff in the organization have strong feedback orientations and exhibit constructive feedback-related behaviors. Steelman et al. (2004) noted that the feedback environment is largely created for a work unit or team by the direct supervisor, thereby implying that many unique microcultures can exist within an organization. The feedback environment is also influenced by peers and colleagues, but most subsequent research has focused on the role of direct supervisors. Those authors expanded on London and Smither's (2002) conceptualization of the feedback environment by identifying seven underlying dimensions: (1) source credibility, (2) feedback quality, (3) feedback delivery, (4) favorable feedback, (5) unfavorable feedback, (6) source availability, and (7) the promotion of feedback seeking.

Steelman et al. (2004) defined the first dimension, source credibility, in the same way that Ilgen et al. (1979) did: as expertise and trustworthiness. They suggested that feedback sources who are knowledgeable about job requirements and performance are in a position to provide evaluative feedback, have motives that inspire the recipient's trust, and will have a greater influence on other people's behavior.

The second dimension of feedback environment, feedback quality, includes the specificity and usefulness of feedback. Steelman et al. (2004) also noted that high-quality feedback is consistent: It does not vary based on the source's mood, liking (i.e., whether the source likes that person or not), or attitude toward the recipient.

The third dimension of the feedback environment is feedback delivery. When feedback is provided in a considerate manner, and the recipient believes that the source has good intentions, it contributes to a more positive feedback experience and to the individual's positive perceptions of the feedback environment.

The fourth and fifth dimensions of the feedback environment are favorable and unfavorable feedback. A favorable feedback environment is cultivated when individuals receive a fair and balanced mix of both negative and positive feedback, and believe that those accurately represent their performance. As noted in Chapter 3, negative feedback is not synonymous with destructive feedback. Negative feedback that is provided in a considerate fashion and helps individuals understand how they can improve their performance can contribute to a favorable feedback environment. Negative feedback is often diagnostic of an individual's performance and can be essential to increasing self-awareness and driving improved performance.

The sixth dimension of the feedback environment, according to the Steelman et al. (2004) model, is source availability, which pertains to how readily and easily individuals can get feedback from their manager or colleagues. Informal, day-to-day feedback is an important component of a good feedback environment; however, managers have to be available for such feedback to occur! Gregory and Levy (2011) found that the mere frequency with which a supervisor and subordinate interacted predicted the subordinate's perceptions of the feedback environment: The more they interacted, the more positive the feedback environment, based on subordinate ratings.

The seventh dimension of the feedback environment is the extent to which feedback seeking is promoted and encouraged. When individuals are encouraged to actively seek feedback on their performance and receive useful and constructive feedback in return, that encouragement helps build a strong, favorable feedback environment. The extent to which individuals seek feedback is often contingent on the reactions and responses to their inquiries. If managers are responsive to feedback seeking and encourage their employees to proactively seek feedback, employees will be more inclined to actively seek feedback (Williams et al., 1999).

Steelman et al. (2004) used these seven dimensions to develop a measure of an organization's feedback environment: the Feedback Environment Scale (FES). Employees can complete the self-report scale about their supervisor or coworkers, and scale scores can be used for the seven dimensions individually or can be combined to give a score for the overall feedback environment. In developing the measure, Steelman et al. found that a favorable feedback environment was related to better supervisor–subordinate relationships (assessed as leader–member exchange), higher satisfaction with feedback, higher motivation to use feedback, and increased feedback-seeking behavior. Those findings regarding satisfaction, motivation to use feedback, and increased feedback seeking speak to London and Smither's (2002) predictions about the reciprocal relationship between feedback environment and feedback orientation, because those behaviors likely indicate an individual's feedback orientation and the influence of the feedback environment. The development of the FES has allowed for subsequent researchers to examine important organizational outcomes, such as employee attitudes, turnover intentions, job performance, and well-being at work (Anseel & Lievens, 2007; Norris-Watts & Levy, 2004; Rosen, Levy, & Hall, 2006; Sparr & Sonnentag, 2008; Whitaker, Dahling, & Levy, 2007). In the past several years, the organizational feedback environment has been tied to an array of critical organizational outcomes, and support has been found in different cultures (Anseel & Lievens, 2007).

Norris-Watts and Levy (2004) found that an organization's feedback environment predicted employees' level of commitment to the organization, which, in turn, predicted the extent to which they engaged in organizational citizenship behaviors (e.g., helping behaviors). When employees work in a developmentally oriented environment rich with feedback, they are more likely to feel committed to the organization and more likely to help their colleagues. Rosen et al. (2006) also found that the feedback environment predicted employees' organizational commitment and that a positive feedback environment predicted higher employee job satisfaction, higher performance, higher morale, and perception of fewer organizational politics. In a favorable feedback environment, employees receive more and better communication about their performance and experience less ambiguity about what is expected of them. Similarly, Whitaker et al. (2007) found that employees have better role clarity when they work in a favorable feedback environment. They are also likely to seek more feedback and have higher performance ratings. Presumably, employees who receive and seek feedback regularly have a better understanding of what they are doing well, where they have room to improve, and generally how they are performing against expectations. As a result, when the time comes for formal performance appraisals, they are less likely to be off course or encounter any undesirable surprises in their formal ratings.

Like Rosen et al. (2006), Anseel and Lievens (2007) also found that employee job satisfaction was influenced by the feedback environment in

A Favorable Feedback Environment	Critical Outcomes Tied to a Favorable Feedback Environment
- A credible source - High-quality feedback - Effective feedback delivery - A mix of favorable and unfavorable feedback - A readily available source - Feedback seeking is promoted and encouraged	✓ Higher organizational commitment and job satisfaction ✓ More helping behaviors ✓ Higher performance ✓ Higher employee morale ✓ Fewer organizational politics ✓ Higher role clarity ✓ More feedback seeking ✓ Better supervisor/subordinate relationships ✓ A greater sense of personal control ✓ Reduced feelings of depression or helplessness ✓ Lower turnover intentions

Figure 6.1

Hallmarks and critical outcomes of a favorable feedback environment.

which employees work. More specifically, they found that a favorable feedback environment led to more positive supervisor–subordinate relationships, which, in turn, led to higher job satisfaction. Sparr and Sonnentag (2008) demonstrated that a favorable feedback environment contributes to employee well-being at work. They found that employees who reported working in a favorable feedback environment had higher job satisfaction and a greater sense of personal control, reduced feelings of job-related depression and helplessness, and lower turnover intentions. In just a few years, research has demonstrated how central the feedback environment is to many critical work outcomes. Figure 6.1 summarizes the outcomes just discussed.

PUTTING IT INTO PRACTICE

To demonstrate how this research on the feedback environment applies to the work of consulting psychologists in organizations, we shift the focus to a case involving Lane, the internal consultant with a Fortune 100 organization, who we learned more about Chapter 3. The organization for which Lane works is a consumer packaged goods company that recently acquired an independently owned manufacturing business that fit nicely with their brand portfolio. The acquisition and initial steps of the integration were completed approximately a year ago, and the acquired employees just had their first opportunity to complete the organization's annual employee engagement survey. Overall, the brand and product acquisition have been successful, but a cursory glance at the engagement survey responses for the acquired employee population has raised some concerns. As part of her role in a practice group within corporate human resources (HR), Lane helps oversee the annual employee engagement survey and is working closely with parts of the business that have less than desirable results to identify and take action on areas for improvement.

The organization-wide survey results have consistently been positive. In general, employees take pride in working for the organization and report strong relationships with their managers, optimism about their future with the company, high job satisfaction, low intentions to leave, and a host of other positive attitudes. However, on examining the results for the acquired employees, Lane finds vastly different results, including significantly lower scores on employee morale, job satisfaction, organizational commitment, relationships with managers, and alarmingly high turnover intentions. Lane knows that it is not unusual for recently acquired employees to have more negative responses than the traditional employee base, but these results are overwhelmingly negative. Lane speaks with her colleagues and with the HR business partners who worked with the acquired business to identify a strategy for taking quick and impactful action that will target these opportunity areas. After much discussion of the options for taking action, the practice group's intern, Julius, who recently finished his master's thesis on antecedents and outcomes of the organizational feedback environment, suggests that they conduct a feedback environment intervention. He notes that all of the low-rated dimensions are issues that are strongly influenced by the organization's feedback environment.

With significant support from Julius, Lane works with the HR business partners to design a feedback environment intervention that targets managers, employees, and the overarching culture. Lane's team invests heavily in training and educating managers on the importance of giving feedback and how to give feedback effectively. They also offer courses on coaching skills for managers to help them cultivate more open and development-focused relationships with their direct reports. Although she believes that rapidly developing the skills of the business's leaders and managers is essential, Lane also knows that these leaders and managers need increased accountability for providing constructive feedback to their employees with greater frequency. Although the training and development programs emphasize the importance of day-to-day, informal feedback exchanges, Lane recognizes that this is a huge shift for a company that has relied primarily on an annual stand-alone performance appraisal for nearly all of their manager–employee feedback discussions. To ensure that feedback exchanges are occurring more frequently, Lane and the HR business partners, with full support from business leaders, establish a new requirement that managers hold quarterly check-ins with each employee. The purpose of these meetings is to share feedback and discuss the employee's current performance and development needs. Although the goal is for managers to provide daily feedback, these quarterly check-ins help ensure that feedback will occur more often than once a year.

In addition to training managers, Lane, Julius, and the HR business partners provide employees with training programs and tools for on-the-job learning on the importance of feedback, including how to deliver it effectively, receive it openly, and act on it in meaningful ways. In the interest of transparency and trust, they directly address the negative organizational survey results and let employees know that their team is working to get things moving in the right direction. Their training programs and tools emphasize the importance of feedback for role clarity and an understanding of performance expectations. They encourage employees to actively seek feedback from their managers and peers and to engage in frequent peer-to-peer dialogues about what is going well and about opportunities to improve and better support one another. In addition, Lane seeks the support of the business leadership (who set the tone for the organization's feedback environment) by having them lead quarterly town hall meetings in which they share updates on the business and encourage employees to ask questions (directly addressing the inquiry and dialogue aspects of a learning organization; Yang et al., 2004). Initial reactions from employees, managers, and business leaders are positive: People seem to appreciate the investment in the business and particularly the employee experience within this part of the business. Lane appreciates the input, but she knows that the best metric will be the results of the next employee engagement survey.

By targeting leader and manager feedback behavior, changing employee expectations for feedback, and providing more opportunities for open, two-way communication, this intervention positively impacted the business's feedback environment. Lane and the HR business partners and leaders were relieved to see double-digit improvements in the following year's employee engagement survey results. Although research has already demonstrated the impact of an organization's feedback environment on employee morale, job satisfaction, organizational commitment, relationship with manager, and turnover intentions, these survey results provided clear evidence of the impact from following a focused and intentional effort at changing the business's feedback environment.

CONCLUSION

The feedback process, which consists of the source, message, and recipient, never occurs in a vacuum. The environment in which the source and recipient work, their past experiences together, the accepted and expected norms for feedback-related behavior, and the actual setting in which the feedback exchange takes place have important implications for how the recipient will perceive, interpret, and act on feedback. For consultants, the ability to see the big picture and understand an organization's feedback environment, what is contributing to it, and how it is driving behavior is essential. Understanding the factors that shape the feedback environment and the outcomes impacted by it will help consultants to identify specific opportunities for change and improvement with their client organizations.

Having explored the core components of the feedback process, we next consider other topics that affect and are affected by feedback: goals and goal-setting, coaching, and performance management.

7

The Role of Feedback in Human Capital and Talent Management Processes

On its own, feedback is a valuable source of information but most often is embedded in processes and practices such as performance management, employee and leader development, and coaching. Each of these processes is inherently linked and relies heavily on giving, seeking, and using feedback. The backbone of any performance management process, feedback provides the critical information and self-insights that drive leader and employee development. Coaches can help individuals work through, interpret, and act on feedback; serve as objective feedback sources; and develop their feedback skills (i.e., giving, seeking, and accepting feedback; developing their feedback orientation). In this chapter, we discuss the role of feedback in each of these processes, starting with performance management.

http://dx.doi.org/10.1037/14619-008
Using Feedback in Organizational Consulting, by J. B. Gregory and P. E. Levy

FEEDBACK AND PERFORMANCE MANAGEMENT

Feedback has been a focal point in performance appraisal and performance management research for decades (Bernardin & Beatty, 1984; Ilgen, Fisher, & Taylor, 1979; Lawler, 1994; Maier, 1958; Murphy & Cleveland, 1995; Pulakos & O'Leary, 2011). In general, the purpose of a performance appraisal is to evaluate employees for administrative (e.g., pay, promotion) and developmental purposes (Farr & Levy, 2006; Landy & Farr, 1983). Unfortunately, all too often performance appraisals end up being isolated, stand-alone annual events that focus on broad, general assessments of employee performance (Pulakos & O'Leary, 2011). Although the spirit of such annual appraisals might be laudable—to provide employees with feedback on their performance to help them understand what they are doing well and where they have room to improve—the timing and delivery of such feedback do not enable real-time changes in behavior and in-process course correction. Moreover, stand-alone performance appraisals often focus too much on the administrative aspects of performance evaluation (i.e., the process, tools; attaining a single numeric rating for an employee, informing pay and promotion decisions, providing data to inform downsizing or layoffs), thus making their developmental value secondary. Research has indicated that traditional performance appraisal systems do not provide employees with useful feedback or set clear expectations for performance (Pulakos & O'Leary, 2011).

An ongoing performance management process provides a desirable alternative to stand-alone, isolated performance appraisals and is unique in that it incorporates various personnel practices, such as informal feedback, goal setting, coaching, and employee development (den Hartog, Boselie, & Paauwe, 2004; DeNisi & Pritchard, 2006). London and Smither's 2002 paper, which we consider a critical building block for our ideas, outlined a model of the ongoing performance management process that emphasizes the importance of feedback for development. They noted that, ideally, feedback "stimulates a positive, development-oriented process that leads, over time, to learning, behavior change, and performance improvement" (p. 88). They also suggested that, in an effective performance management system, individuals use feedback to develop accurate perceptions of their performance and abilities, set achievable goals, and learn and develop new skills. Coaching, individual differences, and context facilitate this development process.

One of the defining features of an ongoing performance management process is the availability of specific, just-in-time performance feedback. Informal, frequent feedback provided throughout the year is more impactful and relevant for behavior change and performance improvement than once-a-year formal appraisals (Pulakos & O'Leary, 2011). Research has demonstrated that frequent informal feedback discussions are associated with strong team performance and are a critical driver of employee performance (Corporate Leadership Council, 2004). In reality, most organizations continue to rely on annual performance appraisals to inform important administrative decisions, such as pay increases, promotions, and reductions in force. Embedding formal appraisals into an ongoing performance management context enhances the effectiveness of such stand-alone events and ensures that employees receive the frequent, informal feedback typically not received in the formal appraisal process. In an ongoing performance management process, if managers are diligent in providing honest, fair, accurate, and timely performance feedback throughout the year, annual formal performance evaluations will be consistent and will provide an overarching summary of employee performance such that employees should not encounter any surprises in those formal appraisals.

For example, if Jennifer's performance rating this year is a 2 on a scale ranging from 1 *(unacceptable)* to 5 *(exceeds expectations)*, the feedback her manager should have provided her throughout the year would have indicated that her performance on specific tasks or activities was unsatisfactory. On the other hand, if Michael received a 5 rating in his formal appraisal, his manager should have provided him with positive, reinforcing feedback throughout the year to communicate to him about his strong performance. It may seem intuitively obvious that employees should not get a negative performance evaluation after receiving positive feedback throughout the year; however, it is also just as important that employees who receive high performance ratings receive consistent feedback throughout the year. Almost everyone likes to receive positive outcome feedback (Medvedeff, Gregory,

& Levy, 2008), such as an "exceeds expectations" performance rating, but employees also need the ongoing reinforcement and encouragement of positive process feedback throughout the year. In general, people need to receive an honest assessment of how they are doing to track progress against goals and expectations and to make any necessary course corrections.

If feedback is the backbone of an effective performance management system, then organizations need to emphasize the elements that contribute to the feedback process and incorporate these elements into their performance management process. Performance management is enabled by a strong feedback environment, managers who demonstrate credibility and deliver feedback with consideration for their employees, messages that help drive behavior change and are delivered in a timely fashion, and employees who are open and receptive to constructive feedback. To enable an effective performance management process, organizations should focus on setting and communicating expectations for managers and employees, and provide the necessary support to managers who bring the process to life for their direct reports. Research has demonstrated that managers who receive training on the performance management process are more comfortable with delivering performance feedback (Bernardin & Villanova, 2005). Simple practice also plays a role: Bernardin and Villanova (2005) found that experience with delivering performance feedback also contributes to a manager's level of comfort with providing feedback.

In addition, being up front and clear with employees about the organization's approach to performance management and the expectations for employees and managers can help support the effectiveness of that system. Research has demonstrated that, when employees understand the performance management process, they are more receptive to feedback, have more positive reactions to evaluative feedback, and are more likely to report the performance management system to be fair (Levy & Williams, 1998). Levy and Williams (1998) found that employees who felt that they understood the performance management system reported higher job satisfaction and organizational commitment. Thus, having a clear understanding of the organization's performance management process drives important outcomes and employee attitudes that impact their day-to-day performance and behavior in the workplace.

If a redesign of an organization's performance management process seems daunting, what one or two changes can be implemented to infuse better feedback practices into the current performance management system? Implementing an ongoing performance management process need not be an all-or-nothing decision. Existing performance management processes can be enhanced by educating managers and human resources (HR) business partners on the importance of frequent, informal feedback exchanges, open dialogue about performance, and an increased focus on growth and development, and then holding them accountable to demonstrating these behaviors.

FEEDBACK SUPPORTING EMPLOYEE DEVELOPMENT

Another attribute of performance management that differentiates it from traditional approaches to performance appraisal is its focus on employee development. In his discussion of ongoing performance management processes, Silverman (1991) stressed the importance of all aspects of performance management in contributing to individual development, including goal setting, frequent informal feedback, formal appraisals, and coaching. Feedback is a fundamental part of employee and leader development because it allows individuals to understand their strengths and their opportunities for development. Negative feedback is particularly valuable for helping people understand their weaknesses and areas in which they have room to grow and develop (O'Malley & Gregory, 2011). Development, like performance management, should not be considered a stand-alone event but, rather, an ongoing process. Hicks and Peterson (1997) demonstrated that systematic HR practices (e.g., performance management) are useful for linking the performance cycle to employee development. Feedback is a vital part of the employee and leader development process.

Research has shown that feedback drives development intentions and activity. Maurer, Mitchell, and Barbeite (2002) found that receiving a desirable amount of feedback drove manager participation in development. London, Larsen, and Thisted (1999) found that individuals who actively seek feedback also engage in more active self-development because feedback helps people know where to focus development in that it indicates skills or behaviors people need to learn or develop. London et al. (1999) also found that feedback made recipients feel more empowered, which can be an important precursor to participation in development activity. According to Maurer and Palmer (1999), receiving constructive feedback can lead to having stronger development intentions (e.g., they reported intentions of engaging in development activities), an important precursor to participating in development activity. They found that feedback was more likely to lead to development intentions when people perceived a benefit to improving performance or developing skills, when they felt a sense of social pressure to act on the feedback they received, and when they believed that they had control over their own development or performance improvement.

Feedback not only helps individuals pinpoint where they may want to focus their development but also provides new self-insights and increases self-awareness (London, 2003; O'Malley & Gregory, 2011). Feedback can help people have a more accurate understanding of their strengths, weaknesses, and how others perceive them. Adopting a control theory perspective and having a clearer understanding of one's current reality allows for a more accurate assessment of the distance between the current and desired state. This understanding, in turn, helps to inform development intentions and actions.

Consider, for example, two managers: Justice and Nia, who have the undesirable tendency of micromanaging their employees. Their respective staff members feel that Justice and Nia are often looking over their shoulders, too closely managing specific tasks and work details, and generally failing to provide employees with the independence, autonomy, and decision authority that they would like to have. However, a major difference between Justice and Nia is the extent to which they recognize this behavior in themselves. Justice, for instance, realizes that she micromanages her employees and is also acutely aware of the effect it has on their behavior (e.g., they feel she does not trust them and then get frustrated and do not take full responsibility for their work, because she did not allow them the sense of ownership). Justice has received feedback—both formally and informally—from her staff and her own manager that she tends to micromanage, particularly when she is under stress. Justice knows this management style is counterproductive, but she has been managing this way for more than 2 decades and is struggling to break the habit and use new and better management techniques effectively. Nia, on the other hand, has a "self-awareness gap": She thinks she is a fantastic manager, that her employees are content and inspired at work, and that other managers should learn to follow her example. When she receives feedback about her micromanaging tendencies, she dismisses or discounts it and suggests that she knows that her employees appreciate her hands-on and up-close style. When it comes time for setting development goals, Justice focuses on learning new management techniques and finding ways to break her micromanaging habits, whereas Nia focuses her development on areas that are irrelevant to her real development needs (or at least what others might see as being her development needs).

360° FEEDBACK

Self-awareness is an important precursor to meaningful development (McCarthy & Garavan, 1999; Silverman, Pogson, & Cober, 2005) and having a strong sense of self-awareness provides clarity about where development is most needed. One type of feedback that can help to increase self-awareness is 360° feedback (Fletcher & Baldry, 2000; London, 2003; London & Smither, 1995; McCarthy & Garavan, 1999), which was introduced in Chapter 3. Sometimes referred to as multisource feedback, 360° feedback can help individuals gain self-awareness by receiving feedback (in the form of numerical ratings and qualitative comments) from superiors, subordinates, peers, business partners, clients, and family and friends. Most 360° feedback tools also include self-ratings, which allow for a comparison—sometimes eye-opening—between self and other ratings. For example, when Sean received his 360° feedback report, he found a consistent gap between his self-ratings and those provided by others—all of which indicates that he underrates his performance (e.g., others rate him higher on most behaviors than he rates himself). This is a contrast to Bailey, who is a chronic inflater of his own ratings. Bailey lacks self-awareness, as evidenced by his tendency to overrate his capabilities compared with how others rate him. One way to think about self-awareness gaps that is often used in practice is the Johari Window (Luft & Ingham, 2004). The Johari

Window is a 2 × 2 matrix that crosses what a person knows about himself or herself with what others know about the person; the matrix produces four quadrants: (1) things known to self and known to others (arena), (2) things unknown to self but known to others (blind spot), (3) things known to self but unknown to others (façade), and (4) things neither the individual or others know about that person (unknown). With respect to 360° feedback, disparities in self and other ratings are akin to blind spots on the Johari Window—things that others see but the individual does not.

Research has demonstrated a number of potential benefits to using 360° feedback. Dalessio (1998) suggested that receiving 360° feedback empowers employees to take ownership for their own growth, development, and improved performance. Furthermore, several researchers have shown that multisource feedback can lead to setting more specific and challenging development goals and receiving higher subsequent performance ratings (Seifert, Yukl, & McDonald, 2003; Smither, London, Flautt, Vargas, & Kucine, 2003). Brutus, London, and Martineau (1999) found that the value of multisource feedback in individual development is contingent on the extent to which feedback is used to set developmental goals. They also found that, for supervisors, subordinate ratings exerted the most influence on development goals. Multisource feedback tends to be most honest and accurate when ratings and feedback are anonymous (Ghorpade, 2000; Waldman & Atwater, 1998) and when the purpose of the feedback is solely for development rather than for making administrative (e.g., pay, promotion) decisions (Dalessio, 1998; Toegel & Conger, 2003). Ratings intended for administrative purposes are often distorted because raters may be more lenient when they know that ratings are tied to reward systems. Inaccurate ratings can be detrimental to employee development because they do not contribute to increased self-awareness or provide an honest perspective on the employee's performance. Not surprisingly, employees who receive inflated ratings are less likely to perceive a need for behavior change (London & Smither, 1999). Therefore, managers or coworkers who are lenient in their ratings place employees at a disadvantage and stifle their growth and development.

In addition, 360° feedback can be even more effective for development when employees work with a coach or facilitator to review and interpret results and establish follow-up actions. Smither et al. (2003) found that working through multisource feedback with an external coach resulted in setting more specific development goals, sharing feedback with others, and soliciting suggestions for improvement. They found that managers who worked with an executive coach were significantly more likely to set specific, rather than vague, goals; solicit ideas for improvement; and have higher subsequent ratings from direct reports and supervisors. Similarly, Seifert et al. (2003) found that working through 360° feedback with a facilitator helped employees develop clear action plans for achieving their goals. Both coaching and following through on action plans are important for linking appraisal or assessment with development (Silverman, 1991). Action plans allow employees to break overall development goals into more manageable steps and can help them figure out how to get started in their development plans.

FEEDBACK AND COACHING

Coaching is another talent management practice that incorporates and helps to maximize the value of feedback. Hicks and Peterson (1997) suggested that feedback without coaching is essentially useless for influencing development decisions. Employees need guidance in interpreting and internalizing performance feedback. According to London and Smither (2002), coaching is one of the fundamental components of the performance management process, because it "supports the value of feedback and encourages its productive use" (p. 87). They suggested that the availability of coaching is a hallmark of organizations that have a strong feedback culture. As noted in Chapter 5, individuals who have a favorable feedback orientation tend to be more open to coaching, and coaching can also help to grow and develop people's feedback orientations (Gregory & Levy, 2012; London & Smither, 2002). Furthermore, London (2003) identified five ways in which coaching supports the use of feedback. First, coaches help individuals set appropriate goals based on the feedback they have received. Second, coaches can encourage their clients to talk with their raters or feedback providers to clarify the meaning of feedback or seek additional feedback. Third, coaches can help individuals feel a greater sense of accountability to use the feedback they have received. Fourth, widely available coaching helps strengthen an organization's feedback culture. Fifth, coaches can help individuals take the feedback they have received and interpret and make sense of it in a safe and objective setting. Coaching sessions can provide people with a safe space in which to practice new behaviors and get in-the-moment feedback from the coach on what is working well and where there is room for improvement.

Coaching can take many forms: The role of coach can be filled by an external executive coach, a direct manager, or an HR business partner. Regardless of who fills the role, it is imperative that the person recognize the value of feedback for effective coaching and encourage their coachee to take full ownership for his or her development, including setting development goals, deciding how to pursue those goals, staying accountable for achieving development goals, and seeking additional feedback along the way. Furthermore, coaches need to invest time and effort in cultivating a genuine and development-oriented relationship with their coachees. Research has demonstrated that a high-quality relationship between the coach and coachee is a prerequisite for effective coaching (Gregory & Levy, 2010; Gyllensten & Palmer, 2007; Hunt & Weintraub, 2002; Smither & Reilly, 2001; Ting & Riddle, 2006). Gregory and Levy (2011) investigated some of the factors that contribute to an effective coaching relationship. They used a measure of the perceived quality of the employee–coaching relationship (Gregory & Levy, 2010) to assess contextual variables and individual differences of the coach (in this case, a direct manager) and the coachee that impact the quality of the relationship, which is considered to be the foundation for effective coaching. Their findings indicated that the most important factors influencing the quality of the coaching relationship are the coachee's trust in the coach, the coachee's perception that the coach felt empathy for him or her, the coachee's feedback orientation, and the organizational feedback environment.

Not only can coaching support the use of feedback, but feedback plays a fundamental role in the coaching process (Gregory, Beck, & Carr, 2011; Joo, 2005). Gregory, Levy, and Jeffers (2008) outlined a model of the feedback process in coaching that highlights how feedback fits into executive coaching engagements from beginning to end. Their model is included in Figure 7.1. They suggested that any coaching engagement begins with a catalyst for coaching (Stage 1), which is oftentimes feedback that the

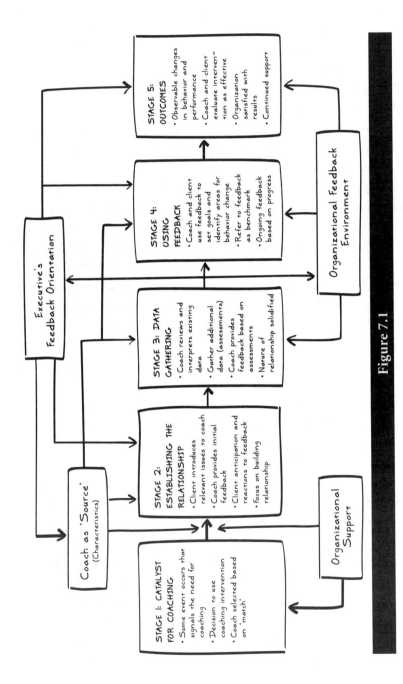

Figure 7.1

The Gregory et al. (2008) model of the feedback process in executive coaching.

coachee has received. For example, Connor (see Chapter 2) received consistent feedback that he needed to develop his executive presence. That feedback was ultimately the driving force in Connor's hiring Helen to be his executive coach.

Once the need for coaching has been identified, the focus shifts to establishing the coaching relationship (Stage 2). This stage includes helping the coachee to see the coach as a credible feedback source and the coach seeking to learn about and understand the coachee (including attributes, such as the coachee's feedback orientation).

In Stage 3, Gregory et al. (2008) suggested that the focus of the coaching engagement is on data gathering through mechanisms such as 360° feedback, interviews, and other assessment tools. Feedback is a critical part of this stage of the coaching process. In addition to gathering substantial feedback from a variety of sources, the coach must also frequently play the role of messenger to the coachee—communicating the feedback that has been gathered and helping the coachee to mindfully process, think through, and decide how to use the feedback. Depending on the circumstances, this stage can be challenging for coaches because feedback—particularly negative feedback—may elicit strong emotional reactions from the coachee and denial or refusal to accept the feedback. The coach must focus on creating a safe and comfortable environment (i.e., judgment free, confidential) that allows coachees to express strong feelings even as they work through and make sense of the feedback received.

Once feedback has been shared and accepted, the focus for feedback in the coaching engagement shifts to using that feedback (Stage 4). Coaches can provide guidance, support, and thought-provoking questions to help their coachees decide where to focus their development efforts based on the feedback they have received and also help them set meaningful and relevant goals. Goal setting is important to coaching, development, and behavior change, and also closely connected to feedback, as discussed in the section on control theory in Chapter 2. Locke and Latham (1990) noted that feedback alone does not drive behavior change. Rather, the goals that people set in response to feedback, and feedback about goal progress, drive behavior change. Gregory et al. (2008) noted that this stage of the coaching engagement tends to be the longest, because behavior change takes time. Feedback can be used throughout this stage of the engagement to gauge goal progress and readjust that progress, as needed.

The fifth stage of the feedback process within executive coaching focuses on outcomes. Depending on the circumstances, this stage can occur concurrently with Stage 4. For example, when coachees set multiple goals for development, chances are they will achieve the more proximal goals while continuing to work toward longer term or more challenging goals. Outcomes from this stage can include increased resilience or self-awareness, achievement of specific personal or career development goals, higher self-efficacy or self-confidence, and improved job performance (Gregory et al., 2008). The conclusion of the coaching engagement should incorporate feedback to gauge the coachee's progress and development, and incorporate feedback for the coach about how much the coaching relationship has supported and enabled that individual's development. Gregory et al. (2008) contended that, overall, coaching engagements start with meaningful feedback that inspires development, continuously draw on and incorporate feedback into coaching discussions and the self-development process, and conclude as feedback provides evidence of development, behavior change, and goal attainment.

CONCLUSION

Feedback is a fundamental part of many HR and talent management processes. It is the backbone of any performance appraisal or performance management system that provides employees with the data and insights necessary to increase self-awareness and drive development intentions and actions. Furthermore, feedback is embedded in the coaching process, regardless of whether that coach is an employee's manager or external executive coach charging $500 per hour. HR practitioners and consultants can add dramatic value to these processes by drawing on evidence-based best practices for giving, receiving, seeking, and using feedback. Direct managers bring most of these processes to life for most of their employees. They typically are the ones leading the performance reviews, driving the day-to-day performance management process, encouraging and supporting employee development, and providing on-the-job coaching.

Consulting psychologists should consider focusing their efforts on developing the feedback skills of managers, who are the first line of contact with most employees. Managers have the greatest influence on the feedback environment (London & Smither, 2002); they convey the organization's values and priorities through performance reviews (Pulakos & O'Leary, 2011), and they convey to employees whether the organization values and prioritizes continuous learning and development through their support (or lack thereof) of employee development activities (Maurer et al., 2002).

In the next chapter, we focus on pulling together the concepts and ideas shared throughout this book, and on providing specific recommendations for using evidence-based best practices for feedback in organizations and with clients. We conclude with some ideas and directions for future research as a way to drive thinking about the importance and use of feedback going forward in the changing organizations of the 21st century.

8

Recommendations for Practice and Directions for Future Research

Feedback plays a critical role in many of the day-to-day actions and activities that consultants face. Feedback is at the heart of communication, self-awareness, performance improvement, development, and motivation, among other things. Understanding and working with the nuances that contribute to effective use of feedback will enhance consulting psychology practices and better serve clients seeking to improve their own or others' performance. Throughout this book, we have referenced our simple model (see Figure 1.5), which highlights four important components of the feedback process: (1) feedback source, (2) actual feedback message, (3) feedback recipient, and (4) context in which the feedback exchanges occurs.

The likelihood of a feedback recipient's accepting, internalizing, and taking action on feedback is contingent on each of these components.

http://dx.doi.org/10.1037/14619-009
Using Feedback in Organizational Consulting, by J. B. Gregory and P. E. Levy
Copyright © 2015 by the American Psychological Association. All rights reserved.

The feedback process is impacted by the relationship between the feedback provider (i.e., source) and recipient, the extent to which the recipient believes the provider is credible (i.e., trustworthy, possesses expertise), and the timing of the feedback delivery. Several aspects of the feedback message—including sign, type, specificity, and focus—play a role in how recipients perceive and react to feedback. Individual differences of feedback recipients, such as their personality, past experiences, motivation, and feedback orientation, color their perception of feedback and the ways in which they choose to respond. Furthermore, contextual variables, such as organizational culture, feedback environment, and the specific setting in which feedback is delivered (i.e., public vs. private), set the tone for how individuals give, seek, and use feedback. Our simple model draws on and distills the takeaway ideas from the foundational models discussed in Chapter 1, including those developed by Ilgen, Fisher, and Taylor (1979); Taylor, Fisher, and Ilgen (1984); Kluger and DeNisi (1996); and London and Smither (2002). Our model is in no way intended to replace those models; rather, it provides a simple, high-level concept with the most essential four components that affect the feedback process.

In this book, we presented cases illustrating how nuances of the feedback process show up in organizational settings, and we demonstrated how ubiquitous feedback is in human capital processes and practices. Chapter 2, which focused on control theory, described Connor's quest to improve his executive presence and discussed his partnership with his executive coach, Helen. By seeking and using constructive feedback from Helen and his trusted colleagues, Connor gained a stronger sense of self-awareness and developed his skills at gauging his own behavior and how it affects and is perceived by others. Drawing on control theory, Connor learned to more clearly define his goal or desired state, assess the gap between his current and desired states, and gauge his gradual progress toward closing that gap. As noted in this chapter, feedback is fundamental for assessing goal progress and the distance between current and desired states (Carver & Scheier, 1998; Johnson, Chang, & Lord, 2006; Vancouver, 2005). This framework—helping clients think about where they are, where they want to be, and the distance in between—can be an effective tool for helping people to put their goals (and what it will take to achieve those goals) into perspective. No matter what the topic of concern, a simple control theory framework can help individuals boil their challenges down to a simple and straightforward structure.

Chapter 3 addressed how research-based best practices for crafting the feedback message can be applied to a 360° feedback report. Lane, the industrial–organizational psychologist in a global Fortune 100 organization, created an evidence-based 360° feedback report that presented feedback messages in a way that helped employees mindfully process, understand, and use the feedback they received. Lane intentionally designed the assessment report to be as developmentally oriented as possible. She made feedback statements more specific and tailored to the individual by linking feedback statements to more specific competency scores. She also ensured that feedback focused on actions and behaviors, rather than abilities or the individual as a person. She built in development tips throughout the report to help individuals think about how they can use the feedback they receive to set goals and drive development activity. By making those changes to the report, Lane found that employees were significantly more likely to use their 360° feedback to set development goals, pursue development activity, and grow and develop.

The case presented in Chapter 4 focused on training managers to understand their important role as feedback providers in an ongoing performance management process. Ted, the external consultant with experience in change management, recognized the value of training managers to effectively deliver feedback to their employees, because they bring the ongoing performance management process to life for their staff. Ted focused on a blended learning program, which included guides, online learning modules, and in-person training and focused on four themes for managers: (1) their role as the feedback provider (the program touched on source credibility—including expertise and trustworthiness), (2) relationship building, (3) the various ways to deliver feedback (i.e., the medium, how to "frame" feedback—such as the situation-behavior-impact [SBI] model), and (4) when to give feedback (i.e., timing, frequency, setting— public vs. private). Through this performance management training initiative, managers learned that the way in which they delivered feedback could make or break the feedback process for employees. As noted in Chapter 7, feedback is the backbone of a performance management process, and managers are generally responsible for providing that day-to-day feedback to their team members. As a result, the effectiveness of a performance management process depends largely on how effectively individual managers deliver feedback to their employees.

Through the case about Sylvia's work with individual executive assessments, Chapter 5 highlighted the role that feedback recipients' individual differences play in the feedback process. Sylvia considered the individual differences (e.g., personality and motivation) of her client, Elizabeth, when determining her approach to their assessment feedback session. At the start of the session, Sylvia invested time in getting to know more about Elizabeth, including her feedback orientation, self-esteem, self-efficacy, and general tendencies. Sylvia used this information to provide additional feedback to Elizabeth, tailored the way she framed her feedback, and set up Elizabeth's executive coaching engagement for success. Sylvia was able to leverage not only assessment data but her observations from getting to know Elizabeth to make her feedback delivery and conversation with Elizabeth more effective. This case demonstrated the value of learning about the feedback recipient as a unique individual—and not simply taking a one-size-fits-all approach to delivering feedback.

Chapter 6 provided a case, involving Lane, about designing and executing a targeted intervention to change an organization's feedback environment. This contextual component of the feedback process was linked to critical outcomes, such as employee morale, job satisfaction, organizational commitment, relationships with managers, and turnover intentions. Lane, Julius (her intern), and their HR team designed an intervention intended to target and improve the feedback environment within a recently acquired part of the business. They focused on driving change through the managers' behavior, because managers generally are the face of the feedback environment to their employees, and provided training for employees to educate them on the value of seeking and using feedback. Those actions led to an improved feedback environment and increases in the critical outcome variables that had raised red flags on the previous employee survey.

These cases illustrated the critical takeaways from feedback research discussed in each chapter. Consultants will find many other ways to incorporate evidence-based practices for using feedback in their work. In the next section, we provide additional recommendations for using feedback effectively in their practice and have divided our recommendations into two categories: those for internal consultants (i.e., who work as consultants or practitioners in a center of excellence, for example, within an organization) and those for external consultants (i.e., who are hired to provide services to a client organization but are not employees of that organization). Following these recommendations is a discussion of directions for future feedback research.

RECOMMENDATIONS FOR PRACTICE: INTERNAL CONSULTANTS

Consultants working within organizations often have ownership or responsibility for key HR, talent, and organizational development processes. They may be responsible for the acquisition, development, and implementation of solutions for performance management, succession planning, training and development, organizational change, recruitment and selection, among other things. They tend to see processes through from beginning to end (or ongoing improvement and revision, because there may not be an end in sight) more than external consultants because they are embedded within the organization. Interfacing with employees and leaders throughout the organization, they secure buy-in and support for their work and align HR processes to the business strategy and priorities. A few processes that internal consultants could enhance with better feedback practices include manager training, employee and leader development, and organizational effectiveness efforts.

Manager Training

A common theme across several cases in this book was the importance of training managers to give feedback effectively. Managers are often responsible for executing key talent management processes and interfacing with employees. To their employees, managers are the face of the organization when it comes to performance management, job assignments, organizational change, and development opportunities. As a result, high-quality manager training that focuses on recognizing the manager's important role in the feedback process (e.g., as the feedback source) can have a substantial impact on the effectiveness of these processes.

Offering a training course for managers on how to give better feedback is a quick, low-cost, and manageable way to improve an organization's feedback culture. Internal consultants interested in offering this kind of program have a variety of options available to them. Many training providers and consulting firms offer this type of program, and consultants have the option of buying an off-the-shelf program or having something customized for the organization, depending on their needs and budget, and on what external partners have to offer.

On a limited budget, consultants can easily put together a short training program for delivery in person or virtually (e.g., via a web conferencing tool). They can draw on concepts presented throughout this book—such as our simple feedback model, the role of the feedback provider, considerations for crafting and delivering the message, and what contributes to employees' reactions and responses to feedback. Consultants could use the simple model as an overarching framework for a short training program. We suggest building opportunities for practice into the training program. After reviewing the basics, engage participants in an action learning activity or have them practice giving feedback to other participants. Straightforward models, such as SBI (Weitzel, 2000), are easy for managers to remember and can help them quickly construct an effective feedback message. Consultants could even consider assigning prework or follow-up to the training, such as having managers actively seek feedback from others or intentionally give constructive feedback to a few people and pay close attention to how they react or respond.

For internal consultants, consider these questions: What effect would training all of the managers to give better feedback have on the organization? What impact would this have on employees' day-to-day experiences?

How would overall stronger manager feedback skills throughout the organization affect the execution of critical talent management processes, such as employee development and performance management? In addition to managers, what impact might consultants anticipate if employees were also trained on giving, seeking, and receiving feedback more effectively? Training could target not only managers but also employees throughout the organization.

Similarly, training on coaching skills for managers can have a dramatic impact on the organizational feedback environment. Gregory (2010) found that manager coaching behavior is highly related to employee ratings of the organizational feedback environment ($r = .79$; $p < .01$), a finding that supports London and Smither's (2002) suggestion that frequent and readily available coaching is a hallmark of organizations with a strong feedback environment. Thus, training managers to use a nondirective coaching approach will help cultivate a positive feedback environment for the organization. As with feedback training, many options exist for buying or building this type of training program. However, as with feedback training, practice is an essential component of a coaching skills training program. Managers must have opportunities to practice their new skills and get feedback (from their practice coachee and even from an observer, if possible) on what is working well and where they have room to improve or better apply their new skills.

Employee and Leader Development

Feedback is essential for development. Feedback helps people gain self-awareness and understand their strengths and opportunities for development, and allows them to gauge progress toward their goals. Regardless of an organization's current approaches to employee and leader development, consultants can use evidence-based best practices for using feedback to enhance current development programs. As noted in Chapter 7, 360° feedback tools are great for helping leaders get a holistic sense of how others perceive them, learning where they might have blind spots in their self-awareness, and deciding what development opportunities will be most valuable to pursue. Implementing a 360° process can be challenging. As with many other tools or processes, consultants have the choice of buying or building a 360° assessment. A variety of consulting firms offer off-the-shelf 360° assessments, which may vary in the extent to which one can customize them (e.g., in terms of items that are included, report formats, who and how many raters can provide feedback, what competencies or skills are assessed). Many organizations opt to create their own in-house 360° assessment based on their unique leadership competency model. Creating a 360° from scratch can be challenging, because pulling together rater feedback and creating a report may require either a lot of manual labor or sophisticated technology. One hybrid approach that many organizations pursue is creating their own content (e.g., assessment items/questions based on their competency model, report content) but working with an assessment provider to host the assessment, create the online interface, and produce assessment reports.

Regardless of which method is applied to set up a 360° assessment, it is important to be mindful of how the assessment will be used. Who will have access to the 360° process? Some organizations empower employees anywhere in the company to initiate a 360° assessment whenever they want, regardless of their level or position within the organization. Other organizations focus use of their 360° assessment on high-potential employees or leaders at or above a certain level of the hierarchy. Some practical considerations for deciding who has access to the organization's 360° process include cost (e.g., the per-person cost of the assessment can be as high as several hundred dollars per assessment) and how the consultant wants to strategically use the assessment (e.g., empowering employees to get and use feedback or using 360° assessment results to inform a high-touch development plan for selected employees as part of a high potential development program). In addition, to maximize the developmental value of 360° assessment feedback, consider training HR managers or business partners to have facilitated discussions with employees in which they walk them through the report. It is important to help employees make sense of the results and to coach them through the setting of development goals and plans based on assessment results.

Good feedback practices will enhance other development efforts, such as mentoring, team building, and the development of employee wellness programs. Mentors are in a unique position to give meaningful, constructive feedback. They should not be in the same reporting line as the individuals they mentor so that their honest, constructive feedback may be less likely to make mentees feel they need to justify or defend their performance—as they might with a direct manager who oversees their work and controls pay and promotion decisions. Equipping employees in the organization who act as mentors with the skills they need to provide behavior-focused, clear, and constructive feedback will enhance their effectiveness as mentors and advisors. Mentors can provide objective feedback and advice and use those to drive a confidential, open, and trust-based conversation with mentees about performance and development, and opportunities to improve both.

Organizational Effectiveness Efforts

Feedback plays a vital role in a variety of organizational effectiveness and development activities, such as employee engagement, strategic planning, organizational change, team building and facilitation. For example, team-building activities include fun or unusual activities not directly related to work that usually take place outside of the regular work setting. Teams that participate in these team-building retreats might have fun and get to know each other better, but team building that focuses on developing critical skills and productive behaviors in the context of the day-to-day work environment may be more likely to translate to actual behavior change in the work context. Having a facilitated discussion with teams about how they currently use feedback and where they have opportunities to improve their feedback practices, coupled with training and practice for giving feedback effectively, is an efficient way to provide team building that will easily translate to behavior change on the job. Internal consultants can draw on concepts presented throughout this book and practices for effective facilitation and team coaching to create a team-building activity that makes a difference for teams and does not take employees away from the office for an entire day or at a substantial cost. At the end of this book, we offer recommendations for further reading on team coaching and facilitation.

Many organizations offer wellness programs that help employees learn about developing healthy habits and provide them access to tools and resources that will enable them to engage in those healthy behaviors. Research has shown that employee wellness programs can lead to lower health care costs for the organization, reduced employee turnover, reduced rates of absenteeism, and higher job satisfaction (Gebhardt & Crump, 1990; Parks & Steelman, 2008). Some organizations are building feedback processes into their wellness programs to help employees increase their self-awareness about wellness behaviors and learn where they have opportunities to improve. New technology is providing biometric feedback to employees as part of those wellness systems. One global Fortune 25 organization, for example, offers a wellness 360° to employees as part of an intensive wellness program. Employees choose coworkers, family members, and friends to complete the 360° assessment and provide feedback on their eating, exercising, sleeping, and work habits. Employees also rate themselves on these behaviors. The assessment report provides employees with feedback from people they love and care about, and helps them identify blind spots where they think they may be performing well, but friends and family members may think otherwise.

One Fortune 500 organization has created an online self-assessment tool that employees can use to get feedback on their habits (e.g., eating, exercise, sleeping), work/life balance, and how well they are using company resources for wellness and work/life balance. Employees complete the self-service assessment whenever they want and wherever they want (as long as they have an Internet connection), and they can choose to keep their results private or share them with others. The assessment report provides feedback on the employees' behaviors, suggestions for improvement, and links to resources to help them take action on their areas for improvement. Although wellness may not be considered a traditional part of employee development, it lays the foundation for employees to perform at their very best.

RECOMMENDATIONS FOR PRACTICE: EXTERNAL CONSULTANTS

Consultants in external roles partner with clients and client organizations by providing their skills and expertise on projects. The duration of these engagements is anywhere from a few days to several years, depending on client needs and the scope of the work. External consultants work on many of the same processes that internal consultants do, such as performance management, learning and development, organizational change and transformation, employee selection, and succession management. As a result, many of the aforementioned recommendations for internal consultants apply to external consultants. External consultants also provide coaching and assessments, and develop tools and resources to support their clients' work. When it comes to feedback, external consultants can help their clients learn to use feedback more effectively, and they can provide candid, honest feedback to their clients regarding their work or the challenges that those clients are facing within organizations.

Coaching and Assessment

Feedback plays an important role in the day-to-day work of consultants who provide coaching and assessment services. In working with clients, consultants and coaches can ensure that they are drawing on best practices when providing feedback to clients—whether that feedback is their own or they are providing feedback based on interviews, assessments, or comments from other stakeholders. In addition, coaches can influence their clients' interpretation of, reaction to, and use of feedback provided by others, including feedback from assessments or formal appraisals, by helping them mindfully process feedback, work through initial strong emotional reactions, and think of instances in which they may have exhibited the behaviors in question. Coaches can help their clients develop a stronger feedback orientation and have increased comfort receiving and actively seeking feedback from others. Helping clients mindfully process and find value in feedback—particularly negative feedback—can begin to enhance their feedback orientation and help them deal with initial negative emotional reactions to feedback so that they can still identify meaningful opportunities for improvement. Because the coaching engagement presents a safe and nonthreatening environment to test out new feedback skills, clients can even practice seeking feedback from their coach.

Many coaches incorporate assessments (e.g., a 360° or other behavior or personality-based assessment) into their coaching practices. Assessment data can be a catalyst or foundation for early coaching conversations. The results present an opportunity to hold up the proverbial mirror to clients, allowing them see how others perceive them and learn about key strengths and opportunities for development based on an objective evaluation. The value of assessment data is maximized when coaches help their clients work through and make sense of assessment feedback by thinking of examples of their tendencies or past behaviors that exemplify the feedback they have received. Clients may struggle to identify next steps for development after reviewing assessment data, so coaches can guide them in identifying their top development priorities and help them set clear goals and actionable plans for follow-up.

Providing Constructive Feedback to Clients

In addition to helping clients infuse better feedback practices into their HR and talent management processes, coaches can provide clients with feedback on their work, ideas, and strategies for getting that work done. Effective consultants seek to make their clients look good to other stakeholders within the client organization. By providing constructive feedback on clients' ideas, projects, and work products, consultants can help clients build skills and increase the quality of their own work. Clients often look to their external consulting partners as experts, objective observers, and trusted advisors. Consultants can build those partnerships by being honest, reliable, trustworthy, and expert sources of feedback who provide reinforcing and constructive input on their client's work.

Using Feedback to Be a Better Consultant

Feedback helps external consultants be more effective consultants. External consultants should make a habit of actively seeking feedback from clients to understand how well they have met expectations, what worked well and what did not in the client–consultant relationship, and how they can provide even better service in the future. This feedback could be provided via a casual conversation or in a more formal scorecard process, depending on the preferred style and approach of the consultant (or consulting firm). In addition, experienced consultants can provide feedback to more junior consultants on how well or poorly they have interacted with clients. Feedback, of course, can be provided on tasks and deliverables, but because client interface is so crucial to the effectiveness of consulting practices, consultants will benefit tremendously from having someone else observe their behavior and reflect back to them their strengths for interacting with clients and their opportunities for improvement.

Despite decades of important research, there is still ample room to further develop evidence-based best practices for using feedback in consulting psychology. We believe that some of the best research is inspired by practice and, likewise, some of the best practices are those with roots in empirical research. In the next section, we provide opportunities for future feedback research. We encourage consultants to pursue research if so inclined; if not, consider teaming up with a researcher who might be seeking ideas and inspiration. Consultants' practice-based perspective will lend useful context and meaning to feedback research, and ensure that it adds value for practice and helps build the body of literature.

DIRECTIONS FOR FUTURE RESEARCH

London and Smither (2002) inspired some of the most impactful recent research when they introduced feedback orientation and feedback environment into the performance management process. Although a good deal of research has been conducted on these two concepts (Anseel

& Lievens, 2007; Gregory & Levy, 2011, 2012; Linderbaum & Levy, 2010; Rosen, Levy, & Hall, 2006; Sparr & Sonnentag, 2008; Steelman, Levy, & Snell, 2004), there is substantial room to further develop an understanding of the antecedents and outcomes of feedback orientation and feedback environment. For instance Gabriel, Frantz, Levy, and Hilliard (2014) investigated the interactive effect of feedback orientation and feedback environment on employee empowerment. They found that when employees have a weak or unfavorable feedback orientation, working in a positive feedback environment can lead them to feel less empowered. This finding is intriguing because positive feedback environments are expected to have positive effects on a number of key outcome variables, including feedback orientation. Perhaps without the necessary level of coaching and support, employees feel overwhelmed by a strong positive feedback environment and are less likely to experience the expected positive development. Individuals who do not particularly like receiving feedback could easily feel uncomfortable in a setting in which feedback is provided frequently and staff are expected both to seek feedback on their own and follow through on feedback that they have received. Researchers could investigate what specific experiences cultivate individual feedback orientation and what individual behaviors or organizational precursors build a constructive feedback environment.

Ample opportunity also exists for better understanding what supervisor individual differences drive feedback-related behavior and contribute to a positive feedback environment. Pears and Elicker (2014) suggested that a supervisor's implicit person theory (i.e., whether someone believes that abilities are fixed or can grow and develop; Chiu, Hong, & Dweck, 1997) will influence their attitudes and actions when it comes to providing constructive feedback to others. In addition, a better understanding of supervisor feedback orientation and its effects on the feedback process are needed. For example, some research has suggested that a supervisor's feedback orientation may play a role in shaping the organizational feedback environment (Gregory & Levy, 2008). Pears and Elicker also suggested that it is not just feedback orientation that drives individual feedback-seeking behavior; according to them, individuals may need to feel a certain readiness or openness to change, a concept that has been identified as important for successful coaching (Hunt & Weintraub, 2002).

Nakai and O'Malley (2013) recommended shifting the usual approach to studying feedback processes and adopting a person-centered approach by, for example, identifying profiles that drive feedback behavior. These profiles would describe individuals based on key individual differences, such as self-efficacy, feedback orientation, and motives for seeking feedback. This approach would allow for an examination of how particular profiles relate to feedback-seeking behavior and the use of feedback. More specific research on how to best develop and nurture individual feedback orientation is also needed. Although Linderbaum and Levy (2010) provided an excellent foundation for understanding feedback orientation, including its correlates, antecedents, and outcomes, many questions still need to be answered regarding how to most efficiently and effectively cultivate an individual's feedback orientation.

Future research should also take a closer look at the role of feedback in coaching. Several researchers have begun investigating the role that feedback plays in coaching and how it can be used most effectively (Gregory, Levy, & Jeffers, 2008; Joo, 2005), but opportunities abound to dig deeper. For example, is feedback provided from a coach as impactful and influential as feedback from a colleague or manager? How, specifically, can coaches best develop their clients' feedback orientation and feedback-seeking skills? Furthermore, because managers play such a fundamental role in performance management, employee coaching, and the feedback process in general, research should continue to expand the understanding of how important the supervisor–subordinate relationship is to these processes. Gregory and Levy (2010, 2011) explored the key ingredients of an effective coaching relationship, and many of these findings can be applied to research that focuses on the feedback process. For instance, Gregory and Levy found that manager empathy, trustworthiness, individual consideration, and how often they interact with employees significantly predicted the quality of the managers' coaching relationships, which, in turn, predicted actual coaching behavior. Because feedback and coaching are so inherently linked, these manager behaviors should also play an important role in the feedback process.

In Chapter 4, we touched on the effects that technology has had on feedback exchanges. Although cell phones and other mobile devices have made life easier in many ways, they also have made it much easier to act impulsively and favor efficiency over effectiveness. Research is needed to investigate the impact of using newer technologies (e.g., Skype, FaceTime, other videoconferencing programs; text messages and instant messages) for delivering feedback. One advantage of always-on technology is that it makes real-time feedback delivery easy. However, feedback providers may be more inclined to act hastily and provide feedback that is not well thought out or presented in the most effective manner. Research should investigate how the availability of technology influences feedback provider behavior, how feedback messages may differ according to the technology used to deliver them (e.g., messages may be shorter and less formal when provided via text), and how feedback recipients perceive and respond to feedback provided via various technology platforms.

CLOSING THOUGHTS

Our purpose in writing this book was to highlight the most relevant and recent feedback research, and present it in a way that it contributes to a consulting practice. Feedback is infused into virtually every HR and talent management process and practice, and applying evidence-based best practices will enhance any application of feedback in consulting psychology. The big ideas in this book would not have been possible were it not for decades of strong, theory-driven, and practice-relevant research on the feedback process and related applications. We strongly encourage partnerships between researchers and practitioners to ensure that research adds value to the practical application of feedback in organizations and that practices are informed by research and empirically supported findings. Opportunities for new feedback research and better application of best practices in the workplace are plentiful.

Please use the model and ideas presented in this book. Our simple model can provide a great framework or starting point for discussions with clients or creating and delivering training programs for giving feedback more effectively. Feedback plays an important role in behavioral regulation, performance improvement, individual growth and development, and organizational effectiveness. It also can improve communication and ensure shared understandings and expectations within and beyond the bounds of the workplace. We hope that our readers will use the information we have presented—and also share it with others—to have better work and personal experiences.

Recommendations for Further Reading

In creating this book, we drew on decades of empirical research and thought leadership. The following are books and articles you may want to consult further. In addition, we have selected a few books you may want to consider if interested in learning more about feedback-related topics.

London, M. (2003). *Job feedback: Giving, seeking, and using feedback for performance improvement* (2nd ed.). Mahwah, NJ: Lawrence Erlbaum Associates.

This book provides guidance and insights for human resources practitioners, managers, and employees on how to best use and understand feedback in the workplace. The book provides a more in-depth look at information processing, multisource feedback, and use of feedback in performance appraisal, assessment centers, and more.

Sutton, R. M., Hornsey, M. J., & Douglas, K. M. (Eds.). (2012). *Feedback: The communication of praise, criticism, and advice.* New York, NY: Peter Lang.

Going beyond organizational contexts, this book takes a multi-disciplinary look at feedback in a variety of contexts and draws on cross-cultural research, relationship and interpersonal applications, educational and public health practices, and more.

Weitzel, S. R. (2000). *Feedback that works: How to build and deliver your message.* Greensboro, NC: CCL Press.

Published by the Center for Creative Leadership, this book provides managers and employees in an organization with actionable recommendations on how to give feedback that is clear and drives behavior change.

Downey, M. (2003). *Effective Coaching: Lessons from the coaches' coach.* New York, NY: Thomson Texere.

Strong coaching skills can help to build relationships and make feedback conversations easier and more effective. The author introduces the GROW coaching model, which provides a straightforward and easy to use framework for having meaningful coaching conversations.

Passmore, J., Peterson, D. B., & Freire, T. (Eds.). (2013). *The Wiley-Blackwell handbook of the psychology of coaching and mentoring.* Oxford, UK: Wiley-Blackwell.

This book includes 26 chapters, each of which touches on a unique coaching, mentoring, and development topic. The chapters draw on the most recent and relevant research and provide recommendations for practice and directions for future research.

Pulakos, E. D. (2009). *Performance management: A new approach for driving business results.* Oxford, UK: Wiley-Blackwell.

Adopting a performance management process that emphasizes frequent feedback, clear expectations, and regular dialogue between managers and their direct reports can be challenging. This book provides clear guidance on shifting to an effective, ongoing performance management process.

References

Albright, M. D., & Levy, P. E. (1995). The effects of source credibility and performance rating discrepancy on reactions to multiple raters. *Journal of Applied Social Psychology, 25,* 577–600. http://dx.doi.org/10.1111/j.1559-1816.1995.tb01600.x

Alvero, A. M., Bucklin, B. R., & Austin, J. (2001). An objective review of the effectiveness and essential characteristics of performance feedback in organizational settings (1985–1998). *Journal of Organizational Behavior Management, 21,* 3–29. http://dx.doi.org/10.1300/J075v21n01_02

Anseel, F., & Lievens, F. (2007). The long-term impact of the feedback environment on job satisfaction: A field study in a Belgian context. *Applied Psychology: An International Review, 56,* 254–266. http://dx.doi.org/10.1111/j.1464-0597.2006.00253.x

Ashford, S. J., Blatt, R., & VandeWalle, D. (2003). Reflections on the looking glass: A review of research on feedback-seeking behavior in organizations. *Journal of Management, 29,* 773–799. http://dx.doi.org/10.1016/S0149-2063(03)00079-5

Ashford, S. J., & Cummings, L. L. (1983). Feedback as an individual resource: Personal strategies of creating information. *Organizational Behavior & Human Performance, 32,* 370–398. http://dx.doi.org/10.1016/0030-5073(83)90156-3

Ashford, S. J., & Northcraft, G. B. (1992). Conveying more (or less) than we realize: The role of impression management in feedback seeking. *Organizational Behavior and Human Decision Processes, 53,* 310–334. http://dx.doi.org/10.1016/0749-5978(92)90068-I

Ashford, S. J. & Northcraft, G. B. (2003). Robbing Peter to pay Paul: Feedback environments and enacted priorities in response to competing task demands. *Human Resource Management Review, 13,* 537–559.

Ashford, S. J., & Tsui, A. S. (1991). Self-regulation for managerial effectiveness: The role of active feedback seeking. *Academy of Management Journal, 34,* 251–280. http://dx.doi.org/10.2307/256442

Atwater, L. E., & Brett, J. F. (2005). Antecedents and consequences of reactions to developmental 360-degree feedback. *Journal of Vocational Behavior, 66,* 532–548. http://dx.doi.org/10.1016/j.jvb.2004.05.003

Au, A. K. C., & Chan, D. K. S. (2013). Organizational media choice in performance feedback: A multifaceted approach. *Journal of Applied Social Psychology, 43,* 397–407. http://dx.doi.org/10.1111/j.1559-1816.2013.01009.x

Balcazar, F., Hopkins, B. L., & Suarez, Y. (1985–1986). A critical, objective review of performance feedback. *Journal of Organizational Behavior Management, 7,* 65–89. http://dx.doi.org/10.1300/J075v07n03_05

Bandura, A. (1986). *Social foundations of thought and action: A social cognitive theory.* Englewood Cliffs, NJ: Prentice Hall.

Baron, R. A. (1988). Negative effects of destructive criticism: Impact on conflict, self-efficacy, and task performance. *Journal of Applied Psychology, 73,* 199–207. http://dx.doi.org/10.1037/0021-9010.73.2.199

Baron, R. M., Cowan, G., & Ganz, R. L. (1974). Interaction of locus of control and type of performance feedback. *Journal of Personality and Social Psychology, 30,* 285–292. http://dx.doi.org/10.1037/h0036662

Baron, R. M., & Ganz, R. L. (1972). Effects of locus of control and type of feedback on performance of lower-class Black children. *Journal of Personality and Social Psychology, 21,* 124–130. http://dx.doi.org/10.1037/h0032099

Basgall, J. A., & Snyder, C. R. (1988). Excuses in waiting: External locus of control and reactions to success-failure feedback. *Journal of Personality and Social Psychology, 54,* 656–662. http://dx.doi.org/10.1037/0022-3514.54.4.656

Bass, B. M. (1985). *Leadership and performance beyond expectations.* New York, NY: Free Press.

Bernardin, H. J., & Beatty, R. W. (1984). *Performance appraisal: Assessing human behavior at work.* Boston, MA: Kent.

Bernardin, H. J., & Villanova, P. (2005). Research streams in rater self-efficacy. *Group & Organization Management, 30,* 61–88. http://dx.doi.org/10.1177/1059601104267675

Brett, J. F., & Atwater, L. (2001). 360-degree feedback: Accuracy, reactions and perceptions of usefulness. *Journal of Applied Psychology, 86,* 930–942. http://dx.doi.org/10.1037/0021-9010.86.5.930

Brown, S. P., Ganesan, S., & Challagalla, G. (2001). Self-efficacy as a moderator of information-seeking effectiveness. *Journal of Applied Psychology, 86,* 1043–1051. http://dx.doi.org/10.1037/0021-9010.86.5.1043

Brutus, S., London, M., & Martineau, J. (1999). The impact of 360-degree feedback on planning for career development. *Journal of Management Development, 18,* 676–693. http://dx.doi.org/10.1108/02621719910293774

Burke, R. J., Weitzel, W., & Weir, T. (1978). Characteristics of effective employee performance review and development interviews: Replication and extension. *Personnel Psychology, 31,* 903–919. http://dx.doi.org/10.1111/j.1744-6570.1978.tb02130.x

Campbell, J. P., & Pritchard, R. D. (1976). Motivation theory in industrial and organizational psychology. In M. D. Dunnette (Ed.), *Handbook of industrial and organizational psychology* (pp. 63–130). Chicago, IL: Rand McNally.

Campion, M. A., & Lord, R. G. (1982). A control systems conceptualization of the goal-setting and changing process. *Organizational Behavior & Human Performance, 30,* 265–287. http://dx.doi.org/10.1016/0030-5073(82)90221-5

Carver, C. S., & Scheier, M. F. (1982). Control theory: A useful conceptual framework for personality—social, clinical, and health psychology. *Psychological Bulletin, 92,* 111–135. http://dx.doi.org/10.1037/0033-2909.92.1.111

Carver, C. S., & Scheier, M. F. (1998). *On the self-regulation of behavior.* New York, NY: Cambridge University Press. http://dx.doi.org/10.1017/CBO9781139174794

Chang, C.-H., Johnson, R. E., & Lord, R. G. (2009). Moving beyond discrepancies: The importance of velocity as a predictor of satisfaction and motivation. *Human Performance, 23,* 58–80. http://dx.doi.org/10.1080/08959280903400226

Chiu, C. Y., Hong, Y., & Dweck, C. S. (1997). Lay dispositionism and implicit theories of personality. *Journal of Personality and Social Psychology, 73,* 19–30. http://dx.doi.org/10.1037/0022-3514.73.1.19

Cianci, A., Schaubroeck, J., & McGill, G. (2010). Achievement goals, feedback, and task performance. *Human Performance, 23,* 131–154. http://dx.doi.org/10.1080/08959281003621687

Colquitt, J. A., LePine, J. A., & Noe, R. A. (2000). Toward an integrative theory of training motivation: A meta-analytic path analysis of 20 years of research. *Journal of Applied Psychology, 85,* 678–707. http://dx.doi.org/10.1037/0021-9010.85.5.678

Cooke, R. A., & Rousseau, D. M. (1988). Behavioral norms and expectations: A quantitative approach to the assessment of organizational cultures. *Group & Organization Management, 13,* 245–273. http://dx.doi.org/10.1177/105960118801300302

Coopersmith, S. (1967). *The antecedents of self-esteem.* San Francisco, CA: W. H. Freeman.

Corporate Leadership Council. (2004). *Driving employee performance and retention through engagement: A quantitative analysis of the effectiveness of employee engagement strategies* (Catalog no. CLC12PV0PD). Washington, DC: Corporate Executive Board.

Corporate Leadership Council. (2012a). *Driving breakthrough performance in the new work environment* (Catalog no. CLC4570512SYN). Washington, DC: Corporate Executive Board.

Corporate Leadership Council. (2012b). *Performance issue root cause diagnostic.* Washington, DC: Corporate Executive Board.

Dahling, J. J., Chau, S. L., & O'Malley, A. (2012). Correlates and consequences of feedback orientation in organizations. *Journal of Management, 38,* 531–546. http://dx.doi.org/10.1177/0149206310375467

Dalessio, A. T. (1998). Using multi-source feedback for employee development and personnel decisions. In J. W. Smither (Ed.), *Performance appraisal* (pp. 278–330). San Francisco, CA: Jossey-Bass.

Deci, E. L. (1975). *Intrinsic motivation.* New York, NY: Plenum Press. http://dx.doi.org/10.1007/978-1-4613-4446-9

den Hartog, D. N., Boselie, R., & Paauwe, J. (2004). Performance management: A model and research agenda. *Applied Psychology: An International Review, 53,* 556–569. http://dx.doi.org/10.1111/j.1464-0597.2004.00188.x

DeNisi, A. S., & Pritchard, R. D. (2006). Performance appraisal, performance management, and improving individual performance: A motivational framework. *Management and Organization Review, 2,* 253–277. http://dx.doi.org/10.1111/j.1740-8784.2006.00042.x

Diefendorff, J. M., & Lord, R. G. (2008). Goal-striving and self-regulation processes. In R. Kanfer, G. Chen, & R. D. Pritchard (Eds.), *Work motivation: Past, present, and future* (pp. 151–196). New York, NY: Routledge.

Dominick, P. G., Reilly, R. R., & Byrne, J. (2004, April). *Individual differences and peer feedback: Personality's impact on behavior change.* Paper presented at the 19th annual conference of the Society for Industrial and Organizational Psychology, Chicago, IL.

Dweck, C. S. (1975). The role of expectations and attributions in the alleviation of learned helplessness. *Journal of Personality and Social Psychology, 31,* 674–685. http://dx.doi.org/10.1037/h0077149

Dweck, C. S. (1986). Motivational processes affecting learning. *American Psychologist, 41,* 1040–1048. http://dx.doi.org/10.1037/0003-066X.41.10.1040

Dweck, C. S. (2006). *Mindset: The new psychology of success.* New York, NY: Random House.

Earley, P. C., Northcraft, G. B., Lee, C., & Lituchy, T. R. (1990). Impact of process and outcome feedback on the relation of goal setting to task performance. *Academy of Management Journal, 33,* 87–105. http://dx.doi.org/10.2307/256353

Elliott, E. S., & Dweck, C. S. (1988). Goals: An approach to motivation and achievement. *Journal of Personality and Social Psychology, 54,* 5–12. http://dx.doi.org/10.1037/0022-3514.54.1.5

Epley, N., & Whitchurch, E. (2008). Mirror, mirror on the wall: Enhancement in self-recognition. *Personality and Social Psychology Bulletin, 34,* 1159–1170. http://dx.doi.org/10.1177/0146167208318601

Farr, J. L., & Levy, P. E. (2006). Performance appraisal. In L. L. Koppes (Ed.), *Historical perspectives in industrial and organizational psychology* (pp. 311–327). Mahwah, NJ: Erlbaum.

Fedor, D. B., Davis, W. D., Maslyn, J. N., & Mathieson, K. (2001). Performance improvement efforts in response to negative feedback: The roles of source power and recipient self-esteem. *Journal of Management, 27,* 79–97. http://dx.doi.org/10.1177/014920630102700105

Fishbach, A., Eyal, T., & Finkelstein, S. R. (2010). How positive and negative feedback motivate goal pursuit. *Social and Personality Psychology Compass, 4,* 517–530. http://dx.doi.org/10.1111/j.1751-9004.2010.00285.x

Fletcher, C., & Baldry, C. (2000). A study of individual differences and self-awareness in the context of multisource feedback. *Journal of Occupational and Organizational Psychology, 73,* 303–319. http://dx.doi.org/10.1348/096317900167047

Förster, J., Grant, H., Idson, L. C., & Higgins, E. T. (2001). Success/failure feedback, expectancies, and approach/avoidance motivation: How regulatory focus moderates classic relations. *Journal of Experimental Social Psychology, 37,* 253–260. http://dx.doi.org/10.1006/jesp.2000.1455

Fredrickson, B. L., & Branigan, C. (2005). Positive emotions broaden the scope of attention and thought-action repertoires. *Cognition and Emotion, 19,* 313–332. http://dx.doi.org/10.1080/02699930441000238

French, J. R. P., & Raven, B. (1959). The bases of social power. In D. Cartwright (Ed.), *Studies in social power* (pp. 150–167). Ann Arbor, MI: Institute for Social Research.

Gabriel, A. S., Frantz, N. B., Levy, P. E., & Hilliard, A. W. (2014). The supervisor feedback environment is empowering, but not all the time: Feedback orientation as a critical moderator. *Journal of Occupational and Organizational Psychology, 87,* 487–506. http://dx.doi.org/10.1111/joop.12060

Garvin, D. A. (1993). Building learning organizations. *Harvard Business Review, 71,* 78–91.

Gawande, A. (2002). *Complications: A surgeon's notes on an imperfect science.* New York, NY: Metropolitan Books.

Gebhardt, D. L., & Crump, C. E. (1990). Employee fitness and wellness programs in the workplace. *American Psychologist, 45,* 262–272. http://dx.doi.org/10.1037/0003-066X.45.2.262

Ghorpade, J. (2000). Managing the five paradoxes of 360-degree feedback. *Academy of Management Executive, 14,* 140–150.

Gregory, J. B. (2010). *Employee coaching: The importance of the supervisor/subordinate relationship and related constructs* (Unpublished doctoral dissertation). University of Akron, OH.

Gregory, J. B., Beck, J. W., & Carr, A. E. (2011). Goals, feedback, and self-regulation: Control theory as a natural framework for executive coaching. *Consulting Psychology Journal: Practice and Research, 63*, 26–38. http://dx.doi.org/10.1037/a0023398

Gregory, J. B., & Levy, P. E. (2008, April). *The effect of supervisor feedback orientation on subordinate perceptions of the feedback environment.* Paper presented at the 23rd Annual Conference of the Society for Industrial and Organizational Psychology, San Francisco, CA.

Gregory, J. B., & Levy, P. E. (2010). Employee coaching relationships: Enhancing construct clarity and measurement. *Coaching: An International Journal of Theory, Research and Practice, 3*, 109–123.

Gregory, J. B., & Levy, P. E. (2011). It's not me, it's you: A multilevel examination of variables that impact employee coaching relationships. *Consulting Psychology Journal: Practice and Research, 63*, 67–88. http://dx.doi.org/10.1037/a0024152

Gregory, J. B., & Levy, P. E. (2012). Employee feedback orientation: implications for effective coaching relationships. *Coaching: An International Journal of Theory, Research and Practice, 5*, 86–99.

Gregory, J. B., Levy, P. E., & Jeffers, M. (2008). Development of a model of the feedback process within executive coaching. *Consulting Psychology Journal: Practice and Research, 60*, 42–56. http://dx.doi.org/10.1037/1065-9293.60.1.42

Greller, M. M., & Herold, D. M. (1975). Sources of feedback: A preliminary investigation. *Organizational Behavior & Human Performance, 13*, 244–256. http://dx.doi.org/10.1016/0030-5073(75)90048-3

Guerin, B. (1994). What do people think about the risks of driving? Implications for traffic safety interventions. *Journal of Applied Social Psychology, 24*, 994–1021. http://dx.doi.org/10.1111/j.1559-1816.1994.tb02370.x

Gyllensten, K., & Palmer, S. (2007). The coaching relationship: An interpretive phenomenological analysis. *International Coaching Psychology Review, 2*, 168–177.

Hammer, L. B., & Stone-Romero, E. F. (1996). Effects of mood state and favorability of feedback on reactions to performance feedback. *Perceptual and Motor Skills, 83*, 923–934. http://dx.doi.org/10.2466/pms.1996.83.3.923

Hanser, L. M., & Muchinsky, P. M. (1978). Work as an information environment. *Organizational Behavior & Human Performance, 21*, 47–60. http://dx.doi.org/10.1016/0030-5073(78)90038-7

Hays, M. J., Kornell, N., & Bjork, R. A. (2013). When and why a failed test potentiates the effectiveness of subsequent study. *Journal of Experimental Psychology: Learning, Memory, and Cognition, 39*, 290–296. http://dx.doi.org/10.1037/a0028468

Headey, B., & Wearing, A. (1988). The sense of relative superiority—central to well-being. *Social Indicators Research, 20,* 497–516.

Herold, D. M., & Parsons, C. K. (1985). Assessing the feedback environment in work organizations: Development of the job feedback survey. *Journal of Applied Psychology, 70,* 290–305. http://dx.doi.org/10.1037/0021-9010.70.2.290

Heslin, P. A., Latham, G. P., & VandeWalle, D. (2005). The effect of implicit person theory on performance appraisals. *Journal of Applied Psychology, 90,* 842–856. http://dx.doi.org/10.1037/0021-9010.90.5.842

Hicks, M. D., & Peterson, D. B. (1997). Just enough to be dangerous: The rest of what you need to know about development. *Consulting Psychology Journal: Practice and Research, 49,* 171–193. http://dx.doi.org/10.1037/1061-4087.49.3.171

Higgins, E. T. (2000). Making a good decision: Value from fit. *American Psychologist, 55,* 1217–1230. http://dx.doi.org/10.1037/0003-066X.55.11.1217

Hillman, L. W., Schwandt, D. R., & Bartz, D. E. (1990). Enhancing staff members' performance through feedback and coaching. *Journal of Management Development, 9,* 20–27. http://dx.doi.org/10.1108/02621719010135110

Hunt, J. M., & Weintraub, J. R. (2002). *The coaching manager: Developing top talent in business.* Thousand Oaks, CA: Sage.

Idson, L. C., & Higgins, E. T. (2000). How current feedback and chronic effectiveness influence motivation: Everything to gain versus everything to lose. *European Journal of Social Psychology, 30,* 583–592. http://dx.doi.org/10.1002/1099-0992(200007/08)30:4<583::AID-EJSP9>3.0.CO;2-S

Ilgen, D. R., Fisher, C. D., & Taylor, M. S. (1979). Consequences of individual feedback on behavior in organizations. *Journal of Applied Psychology, 64,* 349–371. http://dx.doi.org/10.1037/0021-9010.64.4.349

Ingram, R. E. (1984). Information processing and feedback: Effects of mood and information favorability on the cognitive processing of personally relevant information. *Cognitive Therapy and Research, 8,* 371–385. http://dx.doi.org/10.1007/BF01173312

Jarzebowski, A., Palermo, J., & van de Berg, R. (2012). When feedback is not enough: The impact of regulatory fit on motivation after positive feedback. *International Coaching Psychology Review, 7,* 14–32.

Johnson, R. E., Chang, C., & Lord, R. G. (2006). Moving from cognition to behavior: What the research says. *Psychological Bulletin, 132,* 381–415. http://dx.doi.org/10.1037/0033-2909.132.3.381

Joo, B. K. (2005). Executive coaching: A conceptual framework from an integrative review of research and practice. *Human Resource Development Review, 4,* 462–488. http://dx.doi.org/10.1177/1534484305280866

Kluger, A. N., & DeNisi, A. (1996). The effects of feedback interventions on performance: A historical review, a meta-analysis, and a preliminary feedback intervention theory. *Psychological Bulletin, 119*, 254–284. http:// dx.doi.org/10.1037/0033-2909.119.2.254

Krasman, J. (2010). The feedback-seeking personality: Big Five and feedback-seeking behavior. *Journal of Leadership & Organizational Studies, 17*, 18–32. http://dx.doi.org/10.1177/1548051809350895

Kurpius, D. (1978). Consultation theory and process: An integrated model. *Personnel and Guidance Journal, 56*, 335–338. http://dx.doi.org/10.1002/j.2164-4918.1978. tb04643.x

Lam, S. S., & Schaubroeck, J. (2000). The role of locus of control in reactions to being promoted and to being passed over: A quasi-experiment. *Academy of Management Journal, 43*, 66–78. http://dx.doi.org/10.2307/1556386

Landy, F. J., Barnes, J. L., & Murphy, K. R. (1978). Correlates of perceived fairness and accuracy of performance evaluation. *Journal of Applied Psychology, 63*, 751–754. http://dx.doi.org/10.1037/0021-9010.63.6.751

Landy, F. J., & Farr, J. L. (1983). *The measurement of work performance.* New York, NY: Academic Press.

Larson, J. R. (1984). The performance feedback process: A preliminary model. *Organizational Behavior & Human Performance, 33*, 42–76. http://dx.doi.org/ 10.1016/0030-5073(84)90011-4

Lawler, E. E. (1994). *Motivation in work organizations.* San Francisco, CA: Jossey-Bass.

Levy, P. E., Albright, M. D., Cawley, B. D., & Williams, J. R. (1995). Situational and individual determinants of feedback seeking: A closer look at the process. *Organizational Behavior and Human Decision Processes, 62*, 23–37. http:// dx.doi.org/10.1006/obhd.1995.1028

Levy, P. E., Cober, R. T., & Miller, T. (2002). The effect of transformational and transactional leadership perceptions on feedback-seeking intentions. *Journal of Applied Social Psychology, 32*, 1703–1720. http://dx.doi.org/10.1111/j.1559-1816.2002. tb02771.x

Levy, P. E., & Williams, J. R. (1998). The role of perceived system knowledge in predicting appraisal reactions, job satisfaction, and organizational commitment. *Journal of Organizational Behavior, 19*, 53–65. http://dx.doi.org/10.1002/(SICI)1099-1379(199801)19:1<53::AID-JOB826>3.0.CO;2-D

Linderbaum, B. G., & Levy, P. E. (2010). The development and validation of the Feedback Orientation Scale (FOS). *Journal of Management, 36*, 1372–1405. http://dx.doi.org/10.1177/0149206310373145

Locke, E. A., & Latham, G. P. (1990). *A theory of goal setting and task performance.* Englewood Cliffs, NJ: Prentice Hall.

London, M. (2003). *Job feedback: Giving, seeking, and using feedback for performance improvement.* Mahwah, NJ: Erlbaum.

London, M., Larsen, H. H., & Thisted, L. N. (1999). Relationships between feedback and self-development. *Group & Organization Management, 24,* 5–27. http://dx.doi.org/10.1177/1059601199241002

London, M., & Smither, J. W. (1995). Can multisource feedback change perceptions of goal accomplishment, self-evaluations, and performance-related outcomes? Theory-based applications and directions for research. *Personnel Psychology, 48,* 803–839. http://dx.doi.org/10.1111/j.1744-6570.1995.tb01782.x

London, M., & Smither, J. W. (1999). Empowered self-development and continuous learning. *Human Resource Management, 38,* 3–15. http://dx.doi.org/ 10.1002/(SICI)1099-050X(199921)38:1<3::AID-HRM2>3.0.CO;2-M

London, M., & Smither, J. W. (2002). Feedback orientation, feedback culture, and the longitudinal performance management process. *Human Resource Management Review, 12,* 81–100. http://dx.doi.org/10.1016/S1053-4822(01)00043-2

Lord, R. G., & Levy, P. E. (1994). Moving from cognition to action: A control theory perspective. *Applied Psychology: An International Review, 43,* 335–367. http://dx.doi.org/10.1111/j.1464-0597.1994.tb00828.x

Ludwig, T. D., Biggs, J., Wagner, S., & Geller, E. S. (2001). Using public feedback and competitive rewards to increase the safe driving of pizza deliverers. *Journal of Organizational Behavior Management, 21,* 75–104. http://dx.doi. org/10.1300/J075v21n04_06

Luft, J., & Ingham, H. (2004). Johari Window. In A. Lowy & P. Hood, *The power of the 2 x 2 matrix: Using 2 x 2 thinking to solve business problems and make better decisions* (pp. 255–261). San Francisco, CA: Jossey-Bass.

Lundgren, D. C., & Rudawsky, D. J. (2000). Speaking one's mind or biting one's tongue: When do angered persons express or withhold feedback in transactions with male and female peers? *Social Psychology Quarterly, 63,* 253–263. http://dx.doi.org/10.2307/2695872

Maier, N. R. F. (1958). *The appraisal interview: Objective methods and skills.* London, England: Wiley.

Marsick, V. J., & Watkins, K. E. (1999). *Facilitating learning organizations: Making learning count.* Aldershot, England: Gower.

Maurer, T. J., Mitchell, D. R. D., & Barbeite, F. G. (2002). Predictors of attitudes toward a 360-degree feedback system and involvement in postfeedback management development activity. *Journal of Occupational and Organizational Psychology, 75,* 87–107. http://dx.doi.org/10.1348/096317902167667

Maurer, T. J., & Palmer, J. K. (1999). Management development intentions following feedback: Role of perceived outcomes, social pressures, and control. *Journal of Management Development, 18,* 733–751. http://dx.doi.org/10.1108/02621719910300784

McCarthy, A. M., & Garavan, T. N. (1999). Developing self-awareness in the managerial career development process: The value of 360-degree feedback and the MBTI. *Journal of European Industrial Training, 23*, 437–445. http://dx.doi.org/10.1108/03090599910302613

McCrae, R. R., & Costa, P. T., Jr. (1999). A five-factor theory of personality. *Handbook of personality: Theory and research* (2nd ed.; pp. 139–153). New York, NY: Guilford Press.

McKenna, F. P., & Myers, L. B. (1997). Illusory self-assessments—Can't they be reduced? *British Journal of Psychology, 88*, 39–51. http://dx.doi.org/10.1111/j.2044-8295.1997.tb02619.x

Medvedeff, M., Gregory, J. B., & Levy, P. E. (2008). How attributes of the feedback message affect subsequent feedback seeking: The interactive effects of feedback sign and type. *Psychologica Belgica, 48*, 109–125. http://dx.doi.org/10.5334/pb-48-2-3-109

Miller, G. A., Galanter, E., & Pribram, K. H. (1960). *Plans and the structure of behavior.* New York, NY: Henry Holt. http://dx.doi.org/10.1037/10039-000

Morrison, E. W., & Bies, R. J. (1991). Impression management in the feedback-seeking process: A literature review and research agenda. *Academy of Management Review, 16*, 522–541.

Moss, S. E., & Sanchez, J. I. (2004). Are your employees avoiding you? Managerial strategies for closing the feedback gap. *Academy of Management Executive, 18*, 32–44. http://dx.doi.org/10.5465/AME.2004.12691168

Moss, S. E., Sanchez, J. I., Brumbaugh, A. M., & Borkowski, N. (2009). The mediating role of feedback avoidance behavior in the LMX-performance relationship. *Group & Organization Management, 34*, 645–664. http://dx.doi.org/10.1177/1059601109350986

Mueller, C. M., & Dweck, C. S. (1998). Praise for intelligence can undermine children's motivation and performance. *Journal of Personality and Social Psychology, 75*, 33–52. http://dx.doi.org/10.1037/0022-3514.75.1.33

Murphy, K. R., & Cleveland, J. N. (1995). *Understanding performance appraisal: Social, organizational and goal-based perspectives.* Thousand Oaks, CA: Sage.

Myers, D. G. (2010). *Social psychology* (10th ed.). New York, NY: McGraw-Hill.

Nakai, Y., & O'Malley, A. L. (2013, May). *Five faces of feedback: A profile approach to student motivation.* Poster presented at the 25th Annual Convention of the Association for Psychological Science, Washington, DC.

Nemeroff, W. F., & Wexley, K. N. (1979). An exploration of the relationships between performance feedback interview characteristics and interview outcomes as perceived by managers and subordinates. *Journal of Occupational Psychology, 52*, 25–34. http://dx.doi.org/10.1111/j.2044-8325.1979.tb00437.x

Norris-Watts, C., & Levy, P. E. (2004). The mediating role of affective commitment in the relation of the feedback environment to work outcomes. *Journal of Vocational Behavior, 65*, 351–365. http://dx.doi.org/10.1016/j.jvb.2003.08.003

Northcraft, G. B., & Ashford, S. J. (1990). The preservation of self in everyday life: The effects of performance expectations and feedback context on feedback inquiry. *Organizational Behavior and Human Decision Processes, 47,* 42–64. http://dx.doi.org/10.1016/0749-5978(90)90046-C

Nowack, K. M., & Mashihi, S. (2012). Evidence-based answers to 15 questions about leveraging 360-degree feedback. *Consulting Psychology Journal: Practice and Research, 64,* 157–182. http://dx.doi.org/10.1037/a0030011

O'Malley, A. L., & Gregory, J. B. (2011). Don't be such a downer: Using positive psychology to enhance the value of negative feedback. *Psychologist Manager Journal, 14,* 247–264. http://dx.doi.org/10.1080/10887156.2011.621776

Parks, K. M., & Steelman, L. A. (2008). Organizational wellness programs: A meta-analysis. *Journal of Occupational Health Psychology, 13,* 58–68. http://dx.doi.org/10.1037/1076-8998.13.1.58

Pat-El, R., Tillema, H., & van Koppen, S. W. M. (2012). Effects of formative feedback on intrinsic motivation: Examining ethnic differences. *Learning and Individual Differences, 22,* 449–454. http://dx.doi.org/10.1016/j.lindif.2012.04.001

Pears, E., & Elicker, J. (2014, May). *The influence of implicit person theory on feedback environments and coaching relationships.* Poster submitted to the 29th Annual Conference of the Society of Industrial and Organizational Psychology, Honolulu, HI.

Pedler, M., Burgoyne, J., & Boydell, T. (1991). *The learning company: A strategy for sustainable development.* New York, NY: McGraw-Hill.

Pulakos, E. D., & O'Leary, R. S. (2011). Why is performance management broken? *Industrial and Organizational Psychology: Perspectives on Science and Practice, 4,* 146–164. http://dx.doi.org/10.1111/j.1754-9434.2011.01315.x

Raftery, J. N., & Bizer, G. Y. (2009). Negative feedback and performance: The moderating effect of emotion regulation. *Personality and Individual Differences, 47,* 481–486. http://dx.doi.org/10.1016/j.paid.2009.04.024

Robinson, M. D., Moeller, S. K., & Fetterman, A. K. (2010). Neuroticism and responsiveness to error feedback: Adaptive self-regulation versus affective reactivity. *Journal of Personality, 78,* 1469–1496. http://dx.doi.org/10.1111/j.1467-6494.2010.00658.x

Rosen, C. C., Levy, P. E., & Hall, R. J. (2006). Placing perceptions of politics in the context of the feedback environment, employee attitudes, and job performance. *Journal of Applied Psychology, 91,* 211–220. http://dx.doi.org/10.1037/0021-9010.91.1.211

Rotter, J. B. (1966). Generalized expectancies for internal versus external control of reinforcement. *Psychological Monographs, 80*(1), 1–28. http://dx.doi.org/10.1037/h0092976

Seifert, C. F., Yukl, G., & McDonald, R. A. (2003). Effects of multisource feedback and a feedback facilitator on the influence behavior of managers toward subordinates. *Journal of Applied Psychology, 88,* 561–569. http://dx.doi.org/10.1037/0021-9010.88.3.561

Seligman, M. E. P. (1975). *Helplessness: On depression, development, and death.* San Francisco, CA: Freeman.

Senge, P. M. (1990). *The fifth discipline: The art and practice of the learning organization.* New York, NY: Random House.

Shrauger, J. S., & Rosenberg, S. E. (1970). Self-esteem and the effects of success and failure feedback on performance. *Journal of Personality, 38,* 404–417. http://dx.doi.org/10.1111/j.1467-6494.1970.tb00018.x

Shute, V. J. (2008). Focus on formative feedback. *Review of Educational Research, 78,* 153–189. http://dx.doi.org/10.3102/0034654307313795

Silverman, S. B. (1991). Individual development through performance appraisal. In K. N. Wexley (Ed.), *Developing human resources* (pp. 120–151). Washington, DC: Bureau of National Affairs.

Silverman, S. B., Pogson, C. E., & Cober, A. B. (2005). When employees at work don't get it: A model for enhancing individual employee change in response to performance feedback. *Academy of Management Executive, 19,* 135–147. http://dx.doi.org/10.5465/AME.2005.16965190

Smith, R. E., & Sarason, I. G. (1975). Social anxiety and the evaluation of negative interpersonal feedback. *Journal of Consulting and Clinical Psychology, 43,* 429. http://dx.doi.org/10.1037/h0076855

Smither, J. W., London, M., Flautt, R., Vargas, Y., & Kucine, I. (2003). Can working with an executive coach improve multisource feedback ratings over time? A quasi-experimental field study. *Personnel Psychology, 56,* 23–44. http://dx.doi.org/10.1111/j.1744-6570.2003.tb00142.x

Smither, J. W., London, M., & Richmond, K. R. (2005). The relationship between leaders' personality and their reactions to and use of multisource feedback: A longitudinal study. *Group & Organization Management, 30,* 181–210. http://dx.doi.org/10.1177/1059601103254912

Smither, J. W., & Reilly, S. P. (2001). Coaching in organizations. In M. London (Ed.), *How people evaluate others in organizations* (pp. 221–252). Mahwah, NJ: Erlbaum.

Sorenson, J. E., & Franks, D. D. (1972). The relative contribution of ability, self-esteem, and evaluative feedback for performance: Implications for accounting systems. *Accounting Review, 47,* 735–746.

Sparr, J. L., & Sonnentag, S. (2008). Fairness perceptions of supervisor feedback, LMX, and employee well-being at work. *European Journal of Work and Organizational Psychology, 17,* 198–225. http://dx.doi.org/10.1080/13594320701743590

Steel, P. (2007). The nature of procrastination: A meta-analytic and theoretical review of quintessential self-regulatory failure. *Psychological Bulletin, 133,* 65–94. http://dx.doi.org/10.1037/0033-2909.133.1.65

Steelman, L. A., Levy, P. E., & Snell, A. F. (2004). The feedback environment scale (FES): Construct definition, measurement, and validation. *Educational and Psychological Measurement, 64,* 165–184. http://dx.doi.org/10.1177/0013164403258440

Steelman, L. A., & Rutkowski, K. A. (2004). Moderators of employee reactions to negative feedback. *Journal of Managerial Psychology, 19,* 6–18. http://dx.doi.org/10.1108/02683940410520637

Stephens, S. D., & Ludwig, T. D. (2005). Improving anesthesia nurse compliance with universal precautions using group goals and public feedback. *Journal of Organizational Behavior Management, 25,* 37–71. http://dx.doi.org/10.1300/J075v25n02_02

Stone, P. L., Guetal, H. G., & McIntosh, B. (1984). The effects of feedback sequence and expertise of the rates of perceived feedback accuracy. *Personnel Psychology, 37,* 487–506. http://dx.doi.org/10.1111/j.1744-6570.1984.tb00525.x

Strijbos, J. W., Narciss, S., & Dünnebier, K. (2010). Peer feedback content and sender's competence level in academic writing revision tasks: Are they critical for feedback perceptions and efficiency? *Learning and Instruction, 20,* 291–303. http://dx.doi.org/10.1016/j.learninstruc.2009.08.008

Taylor, M. S., Fisher, C. D., & Ilgen, D. R. (1984). Individual's reactions to performance feedback in organizations: Control theory perspective. In K. M. Rowland & G. R. Ferris (Eds.), *Research in personnel and human resource management* (pp. 81–124). Greenwich, CT: JAI Press.

Taylor, S. E., & Brown, J. D. (1988). Illusion and well-being: A social psychological perspective on mental health. *Psychological Bulletin, 103,* 193–210. http://dx.doi.org/10.1037/0033-2909.103.2.193

Ting, S., & Riddle, D. (2006). A framework for leadership development coaching. In S. Ting & P. Scisco (Eds.), *The CCL handbook of coaching: A guide for the leader coach* (pp. 34–62). San Francisco, CA: Jossey-Bass.

Toegel, G., & Conger, J. A. (2003). 360-degree assessment: Time for reinvention. *Academy of Management Learning & Education, 2,* 297–311. http://dx.doi.org/10.5465/AMLE.2003.10932156

Tracey, J. B., Tannenbaum, S. I., & Kavanagh, M. J. (1995). Applying trained skills on the job: The importance of the work environment. *Journal of Applied Psychology, 80,* 239–252. http://dx.doi.org/10.1037/0021-9010.80.2.239

Tuckman, B. W., & Oliver, W. F. (1968). Effectiveness of feedback to teachers as a function of source. *Journal of Educational Psychology, 59,* 297–301. http://dx.doi.org/10.1037/h0026022

Vancouver, J. B. (2005). The depth of history and explanation as benefit and bane for psychological control theories. *Journal of Applied Psychology, 90*, 38–52. http://dx.doi.org/10.1037/0021-9010.90.1.38

Vancouver, J. B., & Kendall, L. N. (2006). When self-efficacy negatively relates to motivation and performance in a learning context. *Journal of Applied Psychology, 91*, 1146–1153. http://dx.doi.org/10.1037/0021-9010.91.5.1146

Vancouver, J. B., More, K. M., & Yoder, R. J. (2008). Self-efficacy and resource allocation: Support for a nonmonotonic, discontinuous model. *Journal of Applied Psychology, 93*, 35–47. http://dx.doi.org/10.1037/0021-9010.93.1.35

Vancouver, J. B., & Morrison, E. W. (1995). Feedback inquiry: The effect of source attributes and individual differences. *Organizational Behavior and Human Decision Processes, 62*, 276–285. http://dx.doi.org/10.1006/obhd.1995.1050

Vancouver, J. B., Thompson, C. M., Tischner, E. C., & Putka, D. J. (2002). Two studies examining the negative effect of self-efficacy on performance. *Journal of Applied Psychology, 87*, 506–516. http://dx.doi.org/10.1037/0021-9010.87.3.506

Van den Bossche, P., Segers, M., & Jansen, N. (2010). Transfer of training: The role of feedback in supportive social networks. *International Journal of Training and Development, 14*, 81–94.

van der Kleij, F. M., Eggen, T. J. H. M., Timmers, C. F., & Veldkamp, B. P. (2012). Effects of feedback in a computer-based assessment for learning. *Computers & Education, 58*, 263–272. http://dx.doi.org/10.1016/j.compedu.2011.07.020

VandeWalle, D. (2003). A goal orientation model of feedback-seeking behavior. *Human Resource Management Review, 13*, 581–604.

Van-Dijk, D., & Kluger, A. N. (2004). Feedback sign effect on motivation: Is it moderated by regulatory focus? *Applied Psychology: An International Review, 53*, 113–135. http://dx.doi.org/10.1111/j.1464-0597.2004.00163.x

Vecchio, R. P., & Anderson, R. J. (2009). Agreement in self–other ratings of leader effectiveness: The role of demographics and personality. *International Journal of Selection and Assessment, 17*, 165–179. http://dx.doi.org/10.1111/j.1468-2389.2009.00460.x

Vroom, V. (1964). *Work and motivation.* New York, NY: Wiley.

Waldman, D., & Atwater, L. E. (1998). *The power of 360-degree feedback: How to leverage performance evaluations for top productivity.* Houston, TX: Gulf.

Walker, A. G., & Smither, J. W. (1999). A five-year study of upward feedback: What managers do with their results matters. *Personnel Psychology, 52*, 393–423. http://dx.doi.org/10.1111/j.1744-6570.1999.tb00166.x

Walker, A. G., Smither, J. W., Atwater, L. E., Dominick, P. G., Brett, J. F., & Reilly, R. R. (2010). Personality and multisource feedback improvement: A longitudinal investigation. *Journal of Behavioral and Applied Management, 11*, 175–204.

Waterhouse, I. K., & Child, I. L. (1953). Frustration and the quality of performance. *Journal of Personality, 21*, 298–311. http://dx.doi.org/10.1111/j.1467-6494.1953.tb01773.x

Waung, M., & Highhouse, S. (1997). Fear of conflict and empathic buffering: Two explanations for the inflation of performance feedback. *Organizational Behavior and Human Decision Processes, 71*, 37–54. http://dx.doi.org/10.1006/obhd.1997.2711

Weick, K. E. (1984). Small wins. *American Psychologist, 39*, 40–49. http://dx.doi.org/10.1037/0003-066X.39.1.40

Weitzel, S. R. (2000). *Feedback that works: How to build and deliver your message.* Greensboro, NC: Center for Creative Leadership.

Whetten, D. A., & Cameron, K. S. (2002). *Developing management skills* (5th ed.). Upper Saddle River, NJ: Pearson Education.

Whitaker, B. G., Dahling, J. J., & Levy, P. (2007). The development of a feedback environment and role clarity model of job performance. *Journal of Management, 33*, 570–591. http://dx.doi.org/10.1177/0149206306297581

White, R. W. (1959). Motivation reconsidered: The concept of competence. *Psychological Review, 66*, 297–333. http://dx.doi.org/10.1037/h0040934

Wiener, N. (1948). *Cybernetics.* Oxford, England: Wiley.

Williams, J. R., Miller, C., Steelman, L. A., & Levy, P. E. (1999). Increasing feedback seeking in public contexts: It takes two (or more) to tango. *Journal of Applied Psychology, 84*, 969–976. http://dx.doi.org/10.1037/0021-9010.84.6.969

Yang, B., Watkins, K. E., & Marsick, V. J. (2004). The construct of the learning organization: Dimensions, measurement, and validation. *Human Resource Development Quarterly, 15*, 31–55. http://dx.doi.org/10.1002/hrdq.1086

Index

About the Authors

Jane Brodie Gregory, PhD, is a senior consultant with PDRI, a CEB company in Arlington, Virginia. The focus of her work and research is on leadership development, motivation, and performance management, with a particular emphasis on coaching, feedback, and goals. She previously was a visiting professor at her undergraduate alma mater, Washington and Lee University, and was a manager of global leadership development with The Procter & Gamble Company, where she led the coaching program and performance management process. Dr. Gregory's research has appeared in a number of publications, including *Consulting Psychology Journal: Practice and Research*, *Industrial and Organizational Psychology: Perspectives on Science and Practice*, and the *Journal of Organizational Behavior*. She completed her doctorate in industrial–organizational psychology at the University of Akron. She is active with the Society for Industrial and Organizational Psychology, the Society of Consulting Psychology, and the Institute of Coaching at Harvard Medical School, where she was a 2010 grant recipient.

Paul E. Levy, PhD, is a professor and chair of the Department of Psychology at the University of Akron. After receiving his doctorate in industrial–organizational psychology from Virginia Polytechnic Institute and State University in 1989, he joined the University of Akron as a faculty member. There, he chaired the nationally ranked industrial–organizational psychology program for 10 years. He is a fellow of the Society for Industrial and

Organizational Psychology and the American Psychological Association. His consulting and research interests include performance appraisal, feedback, motivation, coaching, and organizational surveys/attitudes. He is the author of one of the leading industrial–organizational textbooks in the field and more than 50 refereed publications, many of which have appeared in top journals in the discipline, including the *Journal of Applied Psychology, Organizational Behavior and Human Decision Processes*, and *Personnel Psychology*, and has been an associate editor of *Organizational Behavior and Human Decision Processes* since 2010. Dr. Levy has more than 25 years of consulting and grant-related experience; his clients or sponsors have included the federal government, large private organizations, and local not-for-profit companies.